"You Can't Use Me Today, Lord...
I Don't Feel Spiritual"

A special thanks to our friends, Betty and Fred Hicks of Evansville, Indiana, for their labor of love in the editing of this manuscript.

"You Can't Use Me Today, Lord…
I Don't Feel Spiritual"

by

Steve Sampson

Unless otherwise indicated, all Scripture quotations are taken from the *New King James Version* of the Bible.

"You Can't Use Me Today, Lord...I Don't Feel Spiritual"
ISBN 0-932817-02-5
Library of Congress Catalog Card Number 89-92113
Copyright © 1989 by Steve Sampson
P.O. Box 36324
Birmingham, Alabama 35236

TABLE OF CONTENTS

Introduction

Most Christians I know are quick to admit they have a problem feeling spiritual at all times. This problem has to be confronted, because by thinking in those terms, we limit ourselves from receiving from God. Consequently, when we cannot receive, we rob others of what God could have accomplished through us.

The good news of the new covenant is that God is not influenced or limited by the quandary of whether we feel spiritual or not. He is still God and we are in covenant with Him twenty-four hours a day, a covenant relationship that cannot fail because it is dependent upon His faithfulness and not our performance.

Our relationship with God is significantly greater than being saved and on our way to heaven. We have been made joint-heirs in a covenant union with the Creator of the Universe. It is time to act like it.

Hearing from God should be a part of every Christian's daily experience. These are days when the body of Christ is coming to this realization that knowing God and hearing His voice are not options, but commands. It is not only exciting to hear from God, but of great necessity that we do. "But the people that know their God shall be strong, and carry out great exploits" Daniel 8:32

1

Prayer Answered That We Never Prayed

—A word from God is equal to the manifestation.

"For your Father knows the things you have need of before you ask Him." Matthew 6:8

We were driving back from eastern Kentucky, following several days of meetings. My wife had been complaining for several days about nausea. We prayed hard, rebuking the flu and any type of sickness we could name. However, her nausea only seemed to worsen. Every fifty miles or so I would stop at a gas station or a fast food place and run in to buy her a Coke, as it seemed to be the only thing that would relieve her discomfort.

We continued to pray for several days after arriving back at our home in Alabama, but the nausea steadily hung on. So we finally succumbed to seeing a doctor.

The thought had occurred to us of the possibility that this was a pregnancy, but already having two children at the ages of sixteen and eight years old, this certainly wasn't something we were planning.

The first few minutes in the doctor's office involved the nurse requesting a simple test. While the test was being made, the doctor, who is a good friend of ours, asked us to step into his office. As we sat across from his desk, catching up on recent happenings in one another's lives, I asked him, "If my wife is pregnant, how soon will we know?" He glanced at his watch and replied, "Oh, I think we'll know something in less than a minute." Seconds later, the phone on his desk rang. He picked it up. "Yes?" He said. He paused as he listened to the nurse give him the results of the test. "Okay, thank you," he said. Then as he hung up the phone, he turned and looked at me with a big grin on his face and said, "Congratulations!"

The word rang with a clarion definitiveness through my mind. I could feel the color drain out of my face. My arms felt weak. Surely this could not be reality.

But it was reality. And although we had already begun to suspect that she was indeed pregnant, there was something so final in hearing that physician say, "Congratulations."

We laugh now, but following our visit to his office, the doctor asked us to stop by his house. As my wife and I walked to the door, his wife opened it and said, "Brother Steve, What's wrong?" She knew that we had been for a visit with her husband and thought that I may have been diagnosed with some bad news. My wife laughed and told her how I was having trouble digesting the reality that we were going to have another child. **A prayer was being answered that we had never prayed!**

Although my wife took the news in stride and began to be excited about this blessed event, I had a bit more difficulty. I had visions of my traveling evangelistic ministry tumbling down all around me. I could not comprehend how my wife and I were going to be able to be used by the Lord as a **team** to minister, with a little baby to take care of. Although now I'm ashamed to admit it, I even prayed that it wouldn't be so, but the Lord spoke to me clearly as I prayed. "Stop it, you are praying against life."

Seven and a half months later, Brittani Nicole was born. Never had my wife had such an easy delivery. The Jewish doctor proclaimed "Hallelujah" as our baby girl was being birthed. The presence of the Lord was so real in the delivery room, that there was not a dry eye in the place. I will never forget it.

Our ministry didn't end. God has used my wife's parents who are retired, but full of energy, to come and stay with our children when we go on speaking engagements together. Brittani has been a marvelous blessing to our lives and to our other children, Kristi and David.

WHEN GOD SAYS "CONGRATULATIONS!"

My first reaction that day when we walked out of the doctor's office was that I wanted a second opinion! Of course that was a ridiculous thought.

But I learned something about God. A word from God can be likened to the word of authority of a physician. It is a reality. It is final.

I could have said to my wife. "You don't look pregnant." Or, "I don't see any baby." But we didn't have to see the baby to know there was a baby. She didn't have to look pregnant to know there was a baby. It was a reality in our lives the moment we heard the word, "Congratulations."

We do not possess what God has promised to us as individuals when we see the fulfillment of it. **We possess it the moment the word of the Lord comes to us.** God had already declared Abraham a "Father of a multitude" long before he saw the reality of Isaac. God called the non-existent into existence and it became a reality, before anyone saw it as a reality.

"(as it is written,'I have made you a father of many nations')in the presence of Him whom he believed, **even God, who gives life to the dead and calls those things which do not exist as though they did.**"

Romans 4:17

No woman possesses a baby when she finally holds her newborn in her arms. Long before that she has a baby. The baby has been a reality since conception. That reality is confirmed and finalized when medical tests show up positive and the doctor declares it so. When the baby is finally in her arms after delivery, that is only a manifestation of the reality that has already existed for nine months.

No woman is surprised the day her baby is delivered. She doesn't walk around saying, "What a shock!" She has possessed the baby for months, but now she is **seeing** what she already knew as a reality.

We receive from God the same way. God is a creator. He calls forth life in us. Nothing God says to us becomes a reality when we finally see it with our eyes. It is a reality the day we hear the Holy Spirit declare the promise to us!

God is a God who talks! When He talks, He impregnates us with a promise of something He is bringing forth in our lives. **At that moment it is a reality.**

Jesus changed Simon's name to Peter, which meant a stone or rock. (John 1:42) However, that didn't guarantee Peter would act like a rock immediately. In fact, he seemed to act quite the opposite a good portion of the time. But that was irrelevant to Jesus. He believed what He said already existed! And God always believes what He says, **already** exists! God thinks He knows what He is talking about. We should have the same confidence in Him. His word cannot fail.

SEEING IS NOT BELIEVING

When the royal official came to Jesus at Cana and implored Him to come and heal his sick and dying son at Capernaum, Jesus wouldn't go. Instead He used the opportunity to demonstrate that He heals by His word.

Jesus said to him,

"Unless you people see signs and wonders, you will by no means believe."

John 4:48

Jesus was challenging the people to not have to see Him do the sign and wonder before they believed. He was using this situation to take the people listening (including us) into a higher realm. **A word from His mouth is equal to the manifestation!**

The nobleman still didn't seem to understand and said, "Sir, come down before my child dies!"

(vs. 49)

It was then that Jesus put the man to a test.

"Go your way; your son lives."

(vs. 50a)

Then the Scripture says plainly,

"...So the man believed the word that Jesus spoke to him, and he went his way."

(vs. 50)

The man had to make a life-changing choice. He could have walked away in a rage claiming that Jesus personally prayed for other people, but was unwilling to pray for his son. He could have said, "How do I know that my son is really okay?" He could have insisted on several confirmations, as many of us do anytime God speaks to us.

But this royal official made a decision to believe! He

11

recognized that Jesus was equal to His word. The word from His mouth equated the manifestation.

> "And as he was going down, his servants met him and told him, saying, 'Your son lives!' Then he inquired of them the hour when he got better. And they said to him, 'Yesterday at the seventh hour the fever left him.' So the father knew that it was at the same hour in which Jesus said to him, 'Your son lives.' And he himself believed, and his whole household."
>
> (vs.51-53)

Imagine the joy of that household!

The moment this man made the decision to believe the word of Jesus, and acted on his belief by turning to go home, faith was conceived and the fever had to leave.

GOD AND HIS WORD ARE ONE

One year our son was within three weeks of his birthday. Every evening I would watch him in bed before he turned the lights out going through the various catalogues, and "enjoying" the gifts he was going to receive. He was having the best time! Suddenly I recognized his line of thinking. Why wait to enjoy his birthday which was a long three weeks away? He would just go ahead and enjoy it now! The Lego sets and other gifts he had asked for were already a reality to him, because he was so confident that he would receive what he asked for on his birthday.

God desires us to be so confident of His promises and provision and His faithfulness, that we act as if it is already so before we see it as so.

On one occasion I promised my son that I would take him to Disneyworld. From the moment I promised him, he was crazy with excitement, even though the trip was weeks away. My word of promise was a reality to him, and was as good as being there. He rejoiced each day as if he was already there enjoying it. It was just as real to him then, as the day we were finally there being trampled by multitudes of people.

When the Lord gives His word to us, concerning something He is going to bring about in our lives, that promise is a reality. It doesn't matter if the circumstances change immediately, because what He says already exists! He is equal to His Word.

ACT AS IF IT IS ALREADY SO!

What does God require of us in the new covenant? Before we receive anything, act as if it is already so!

Young businessmen who are starting out in the business world are told by their companies to act successful and to dress successful, even if they have to go in debt to do it. The companies see the importance of their salesmen projecting a successful image. Few potential sales are closed with clients if the salesman looks and acts like a loser. No one wants his money handled by someone who looks as if he has never been able to manage his own.

We are God's representatives on earth. We are ambassadors for Him. We must live in the reality of His goodness. A cheerful countenance and a joyful and confident spirit glorify God. My favorite bumper sticker says, "I refuse to gratify the devil by being discouraged." Acting as if victory is so, even if it doesn't seem to be so, brings forth the reality quickly that it **is so**. Sometimes we have to command our soul to praise the Lord. David said,

> "Why are you cast down, O my soul? And why are you dis-quieted within me? **Hope in God**; For I shall yet praise Him, the help of my countenance and my God."
>
> Psalm 42:11

When Isaiah prophesied to the barren woman, the command from the Spirit of God was to rejoice as if it were already so. While she was still in her barren state, the barren woman was to rejoice. The prophetic directive was not to rejoice when she saw herself fruitful, but to rejoice in faith while still feeling fruitless and barren. After all, who can't rejoice when one sees the manifestation?

The singing and rejoicing would cause fruitfulness. Rejoicing causes the barren to become fruitful. It prepares the soil of the heart to receive the life-giving word of the Lord. Rejoicing is believing it to be so. Rejoicing is acting as if it is already so.

> "'Sing, O barren, You who have not borne! Break forth into singing, and cry aloud, You who have not travailed with child! For more are the children of the desolate than the children of the married woman,' says the Lord."
>
> Isaiah 54:1

I always know when my children believe me when I give them my word. They rejoice. Although they do not see, they rejoice in my word. Complaining is always indicative of unbelief. Rejoicing is always indicative of believing. Complaining is only enduring with no intention of believing or learning anything.

OUR PROBLEM IS NOT WITH THE WRITTEN WORD, BUT WITH THE SPOKEN WORD

Most Christians would be willing to fight over the validity of the Word of God. We carry our Bible with us, have it next to our beds at night, and treasure every word within it. But that is not where our problem lies.

Zacharias and Elizabeth were model Jews. "And they were both righteous before God, walking in all the commandments and ordinances of the Lord blameless."

But one day when Zecharias was in the temple serving as priest and offering incense, the angel of the Lord appeared to him declaring good news.

"But the angel said to him, 'Do not be afraid, Zacharias, for your prayer is heard; and your wife Elizabeth will bear you a son, and you shall call his name John...' "

Luke 1:13

And after the angel, Gabriel, finishes prophesying all about the Child and his ministry, Zecharias responds by questioning the word and the ability of God to bring it about,

"And Zecharias said to the angel, 'How shall I know this? For I am an old man, and my wife is well advanced in years.' "

(vs. 18)

He gave Gabriel and God a little "unknown information" by telling them that he and his wife were too old to be such instruments in God's hand.

Zecharias was such an upright and ·devout man, and as any person who is committed to God, he would never have rejected the Bible, as it is the written word of God.

But when the **spoken word** came to him, he had a problem with it. Even though it was a personal prophetic utterance from God, and even delivered by an angel, he still questioned it! Why? It did not agree with his natural analytical reasoning!

How many times do we dismiss or reject the good news that God brings to us, simply because it will not fit into our mental computer? The devil is not our problem as much as our rationalizing, analytical minds are our problem. Our minds were not created to filter and scrutinize what God says. His word is already pure. The intellect must become a servant, if we want to walk in intellect must become a servant, if we want to walk in obedience to God.

There is anger and disgust in Gabriel's reaction. He is appalled at the unbelief. (Seems even though we are righteous, we can still have a problem with unbelief).

> "And the angel answered and said to him, 'I am Gabriel, who stands in the presence of God, and was sent to speak to you and bring you these glad tidings. But behold, you will be mute and not be able to speak until the day these things take place, because you did not believe **my words** which will be fulfilled in their own time.' "
>
> (vs. 19-20)

Of course God was not intimidated by Zecharias's unbelief. He intended to fulfill His plan by bringing John the Baptist forth. But Zecharias's unbelief made him mute. He could not speak for the duration of the pregnancy. How many times does our unbelief, which is solely caused by too much thinking, make us mute? Mute people cannot be an effective mouthpiece for God.

As with Zecharias, our problem is not with the written record of the Word of God, but with the active spoken oracle that God speaks.

We must hear a current and fresh word from God, or we will have no life flowing through us. No one sells newspapers that are a week old. Who would buy them? We need to have a fresh word from God. That is the only way we will impart life to anyone. All else is leftovers, and we become like a cassette player, parroting something we've heard someone else say. Without His anointing, it's religious fluff.

2

From the Presence
to the Power

—Power comes from living in His presence.

"They did not remember His power: The day when He redeemed them from the enemy, when he worked His signs in Egypt, and His wonders in the field of Zoan." Psalm 78:42-43

"For our gospel did not come to you in word only, but also in **power...**" I Thessalonians 1:5

"...not with persuasive words of human wisdom, but in **demonstration of the Spirit and of power.** I Corinthians 2:4

My wife was flipping through the Bible one Thursday morning and came across Psalm 78. This chapter is filled with the accounts of God's awesome deeds for Israel. As she read again the description of miracles and divine intervention, of the dividing of the sea, the protection of the cloud by day and the fire by night, the water out of the rock, and the manna from heaven, her eyes fell on verse forty two, **"They did not remember His power: The day when He redeemed them from the hand of the enemy."**

As she read these words, the presence of the Lord overwhelmed her, and she began to cry. Knowing that the Lord was speaking to her, she immediately began to pray and inquire of Him. "How can we know your power?" Immediately He spoke to her, **"I'll move through the**

fruitful vine." She continued to pray, asking "Who is the fruitful vine? Again He spoke to her inaudibly, but with clarion distinctiveness, **"Those who have paid the price to know Me."** She was intently aware of the Lord's emphasis on the words,"to know Me." It was not a question of paying the price to serve Him or to work for Him, but to **know** Him. Again she asked Him, "What keeps us from knowing you?" The Lord said to her, **"Self-satisfaction and distractions."**

THE PROBLEM WITH SELF-SATISFACTION

Self-satisfaction ties God's hands from doing more in our lives. When we cease to desire more from God than what we have in our present experience, we will see Him do little.

Self-satisfaction is a sister to self-centeredness. We quench the flow of God in our lives by an attitude that says, "I don't need anything right now." But we are always in need of God, of His presence and His power— not only for our benefit, but for the benefit of others.

God never performs a miracle just for you personally, but that the miracle will have an effect on the lives of others. His purpose being that the Holy Spirit's flow will be perpetual and have an influence on many people.

That is why self-centeredness and self-satisfaction are so abhorrent to God. When we think we need nothing, we automatically cut off anyone else that could have been ministered to as a result of what God did for us.

PULL SOMETHING OUT OF GOD

We must live with desire...desire toward God. We should be compelled to live with expectancy and dependence on God, that puts a continual demand on His presence.

It is up to us to avail ourselves to God, expecting Him to do more in our lives daily, so that our experiences would provoke and challenge others to desire more of Him.

Whether or not we like to admit it, we are always having an influence on other people. A psychologist who worked with a large American corporation did a study which concluded that every person living a normal lifespan will influence in a major way a minimum of at least 160 people.

We will influence people. The question is, in what direction will we influence them? We minister what we are. No one gets encouraged without encouraging others. No one backslides without taking others with him.

The problem with self-satisfaction is an attitude that develops of "I don't care whether God moves or not." This type of temperament destroys expectation and is the epitome of self-centeredness. There is no doubt that we frustrate the Spirit of God with this type of thinking, and thus prevent Him from doing the miraculous. No parent or grandparent wants to bless children with things when they are not desired and appreciated.

God so desires to do awesome things in us and for us and through us, but we must desire Him to do so with all of our hearts; not only for ourselves, but with an unselfish desire that others may be blessed as well.

Miracles are available in abundance, but unless we pull them out of God, we will see little happen.

Self-satisfaction not only destroys expectation, it quenches the Spirit. It is truly our enemy and an enemy of God.

THE PROBLEM OF DISTRACTIONS

Distractions prevent us from knowing God. No matter how sincere our intentions, they will attempt to usurp our commitment to seek God and give ourselves more to prayer. An old saying is "The road to hell is paved with good intentions." Distractions must be seen as an enemy to diligence, because no matter how good the intentions, they will attempt to thwart and obstruct our determination.

Distractions will keep us from experiencing the genuine presence of God. **Anything** that takes priority in our lives over living in the glorious presence of God, is a distraction.

KNOWING GOD

All ministry should be directed to teaching people to know God. The reason many church pews are filled with dwarf Christians is that we have taught people to seek for knowledge in and of itself, rather that to seek to know God.

God's emphasis is on knowing Him, which results in becoming like Him, His very nature and character manifested within us. If we are full of knowledge but are not Christlike, little has been accomplished.

> "...Knowledge puffs up, but love edifies."
>
> I Corinthians 8:1b

When Hosea prophesied, "My people are destroyed for a lack of knowledge," it was not a lack of information ' or Biblical facts, but a knowledge of **God Himself.** Every experience we have is to bring us to a knowledge of God, that we understand and know His ways.

> "...Because you have rejected knowledge, I also will reject you from being priest for me..."
>
> Hosea 4:6.

God was not saying that they rejected facts or didn't receive good Bible teachers, but that they rejected knowledge of Him—intimacy with Him.

We will never know God, or minister as a priest for Him without being intimate with Him. We must want God Himself more than anything else, including a ministry.

The only way children can be conceived is out of intimacy. The only way to bring forth fruit in God is through intimacy with Him. If our relationship with God is only platonic and casual, there will be no fruit birthed for the kingdom of God.

Jesus declared that many would proclaim on judgment day what great things they had done in His name.

> "Not everyone who says to me, 'Lord, Lord,' shall enter the kingdom of heaven, but he who does the will of My Father in heaven. Many will say to Me in that day, 'Lord, Lord, have we not prophesied in Your name, cast out demons in Your name and done many wonders in Your name?' And then I will declare to them, 'I never knew you; depart from Me, you who practice lawlessness!'"
>
> Matthew 7:21-23

Although they had done many Biblical actions, He rejected them because they did not do it in correspondence with His voice and out of intimacy with Him. In a sense, He was saying, "You never let me control your heart. You would not let Me deal with you, and show Myself to you." It was as a husband saying to his wife, "Although we were legally married, you seldom let me be intimate with you."

A DISTRACTED CHURCH

Someone phrased it well, "God doesn't move in a

21

church; a church moves in God." God always waits upon us to move into Him.

The Laodecian church was a distracted church. They were distracted from fellowship with God to the point of deception. While they thought they had reached the ultimate, they were distracted to the point of blindness. Their own perception was they were in need of nothing.

But His evaluation needed no interpretation.

"Because you say, 'I am rich, and have become wealthy, and have need of nothing'—and **do not know** that you are wretched, miserable, poor, blind, and naked."

Rev. 3:17

A frequently quoted verse comes out of the invitation for repentance to this church, but many have used the verse to relate to sinners. However, Jesus wasn't talking to sinners! He was talking to Spirit-filled, prophesying, tongue-talking, Bible-carrying, cassette-library owning, church-attending, Charismatic Christians, saying,

"Behold, I stand at the door and knock. If anyone hears My voice and opens the door, I will come in to him and dine with him, and he with Me."

(vs. 20)

He was standing at the door seeking fellowship (again) with them. He wasn't saying "Sinner's repent!" He was saying "Christian's repent!" and pleading with them to let Him back into their lives.

No doubt they had all the right motions and programs and ministries and were breaking attendance records—**but no one was learning to know God!**

They were not even aware that He was outside.

They were not living, but existing. To them, and to all distracted and preoccupied Christians He commands,

> "As many as I love, I rebuke and chasten. Therefore be zealous and repent."
>
> (vs.19)

Be zealous toward Him and repent from any distraction that averts you from being intimate with Him.

A CURRENT WORD

If we expect God to anoint us and give life to what we are saying, **we must say what He is saying.**

The reason for lack of life and anointing on preaching is simply that it is not what God is saying for that time. It is not a current word.

Preaching or hearing a sermon doesn't mean we've heard God. The price to pay is to live in the presence of God with a prioritized life of learning His ways. David prayed,

> "Show me Your ways, O Lord; Teach me Your paths. Lead me in Your truth and teach me, For you are the God of my salvation; On You I wait all the day."
>
> Psalm 25:4-5

Man was created to live by listening. In order to have life and to give life, we must hear what is proceeding from the mouth of God. Sermons are a poor substitute for having a fresh word from the Lord.

> "...Man shall not live by bread alone; but man lives by every word that proceeds from the mouth of the Lord."
>
> Deuteronomy 8:3

GOD'S HIGHEST PRIORITY FOR YOU

Eternal life is not seeing how much we can do for God in as little time as possible. Eternal life is the beginning of life in God and coming to know Him.

> "And this is eternal life, that they may **know** You, the only true God, and Jesus Christ whom You have sent."
>
> John 17:3

The absolute highest priority for every Christian, far above any ministry or calling, is to come to know God. Those who do not know God, have little to give to anyone. Without a daily recognition of the voice of the Lord, we deceive ourselves by living a life that is not in tune with the Spirit.

> But let him who glories glory in this, that he **understands and knows Me**, that I am the Lord, exercising lovingkindness, judgment and righteousness in the earth, for in these I delight, says the Lord."
>
> Jeremiah 9:24

Notice He does not say, "Let him who glories glory in this, that he understands the entire book of Revelation."

BE RESPONSIVE TO GOD

No one can be a Christian on His own. That is obvious. But neither can we serve God on our own, we must have the help of the Holy Spirit. We have to learn to live in His presence. Jesus said,

> "Abide in Me, and I in you. As the branch cannot bear fruit of itself, unless it abides in the vine, neither can you, unless you abide in Me. I am the Vine, you are the branches. He who abides in Me, and I in him, bears much fruit; for without Me you can do **nothing.** "
>
> John 15:4-5

Notice He does **not** say, "Without Me you can only do a few things."

When we abide in God, we abide in His presence. As the Scripture says, "For in Him we live and move and have our being..." Acts 17:28 One aspect of maturity is to learn to recognize and respond to the presence of the

Lord. The Bible exhorts us to live close to the Lord, and not to be slow or stubborn about drawing near to Him.

> "Do not be like the horse or like the mule, which have no understanding, which must be harnessed with bit and bridle, **else they will not come near to you.**"
>
> Psalm 32:9

God should not have to use drastic circumstances to get our attention, although sometimes it seems that is the only way He can get us to call upon Him. The Holy Spirit within us is faithful to guide us, but we must be faithful to listen to Him. When we don't listen, then we have to be harnessed with the bit and bridle of circumstances in order to come near to Him.

WHAT DID YOU LEARN?

Several years ago I saw an ad in the paper. A car was for sale that was very reasonably priced. We desperately needed a second car, and knowing the value of used cars with low mileage and this make, I concluded this car to be a real deal. Although deep in my inner man I began to feel an uneasiness, I just couldn't let go of the car with my mind. I viewed it quickly on the way to the airport, while standing in the rain. It was because it was raining that I didn't see that the car was two slightly different colors. I went ahead and bought it and had it delivered to my home.

When I returned home from my trip a week later, I was appalled at what I saw. My heart sank as it became obvious that the car had been repainted due to a major collision. In fact as I looked closer, I could see where the back half of the car had been removed and half of another car had been welded to it.

I was sick inside, and there was no question that I had missed God, by a mile. But all I could hear the Lord saying, was, "What did you learn?" For days that question stayed with me. The Lord wasn't concerned about the financial loss, at least certainly not to the degree that I was. His concern was what I learned out of the experience.

As soon as I admitted to God that I had ignored His voice and relied on my own emotions, He began to give me peace. That wonderful peace reminded me that once we "plead guilty," He is able to redeem anything.

Within a few days I felt directed to take the car to a certain dealership. They worked with me and were willing to pay me a reasonable price for this wrecked car. God turned it into good as I ended up with a more suitable car. Even though I lost money, it could have been much worse. God blessed me, as soon as I admitted what I learned.

Every time I choose not to listen to the voice of the Lord I experience pain. It is not God's will that I have pain, but it is His will that I listen. God will teach us one of two ways. We can learn of Him as we listen to His voice, or if we are too stubborn to listen, we will learn by pain. I recommend listening. That is how we go from His presence to His power.

PRAYER POWER

One day my wife asked the Lord while in prayer, "What is the purpose of praying in tongues? The Lord spoke to her, "It dispels darkness and commands light." That has always stayed with me. The prayer language cuts through all confusion and darkness. We are praying the exact will of God. (Romans 8:26-27) Most people I know who pray in the Spirit, believe that the devil cannot understand the prayer language. Not only does it bypass our minds (unless God gives the interpretation) but it also bypasses the network of the enemy. No wonder the devil is against it! In prayer we can touch the heart of God, and Satan is helpless. Some don't like the idea of anything they cannot understand. But the blessing is, it is the one gift that we cannot defile! Because everything we do understand, we defile, by adding to it or taking away from it.

> "For he who speaks in a tongue does not speak to men but to God, for no one understands him; however, in the spirit he speaks mysteries."
>
> I Corinthians 14:2

Thank God for a prayer language that bypasses our scrutinizing minds. Through it we know the presence of God (you can't pray in the Spirit long before recognizing the presence of the Lord) and hence, taste of His power.

LIVING IN THE PRESENCE OF THE LORD

Before I fully comprehended what it meant to live in the presence of the Lord, I always used to seek God for a sermon topic to preach. But now I have learned, not to seek sermons, but to seek God. In fact I've often wondered if God didn't say to Himself, "It must be Saturday night, because there is Sampson in prayer again, needing a sermon for Sunday."

God has called us to abide in His presence. We don't need to grasp for sermon topics if we abide in His Word. Our life can become a spontaneous flow of hearing what the Spirit is saying, as we meditate on His word day and night. How do we meditate on His Word day and night? The same way we used to meditate on our problems day and night—just never stop thinking and talking about them.

> "My son, give attention to my words; Incline your ear to My

sayings. Do not let them depart from your eyes; keep them in the midst of your heart."

Proverbs 4:20-21

"But his delight is in the law of the Lord, and in His law he meditates day and night."

Psalm 1:2

"This book of the Law shall not depart from your mouth, but you shall meditate in it day and night..."

Joshua 1:8

3

You Don't Need Faith, You Need Vision

—The question is not what God can do for you, but
what He can do **with** you.

"Without a vision, the people perish."   Proverbs 29:18

It was a Saturday morning when I went out into
our single-car garage. It was the first home that we
owned (along with the bank) and parked in the garage
was my 1930 Model A Ford pickup that I had purchased
when I was fourteen years old, for only fifty dollars.

Over the years I had tinkered with it off and on. But
although I had rebuilt the engine, much of the old relic
was still a mess. My father had been kind enough to
transport it down to Beaumont, Texas, for me from
Lincoln, Nebraska, where I grew up.

Now in my late twenties and pastoring my first
church, something seemed almost unrighteous to me for
that project to still be unfinished. As I walked around the
old Ford that morning, surveying the awesome project
ahead, I heard myself speaking outloud to the dilapidated
truck with its parts scattered all over the garage. "I
command this mountain to be removed!" It felt so good
that I said it again...and again. "I command this
mountain to be removed." Peace flooded my being. A
knowledge began to arise in my spirit that God was
moving. I felt excited. It is hard to explain, but I had a
sense that God was excited too.

Within twenty-four hours, a man in our church came to me. "Pastor," he said, " I'll be happy to lend you my tools and part of the use of my shop if you want to go ahead and finish that truck." This auto-body repairman had no knowledge of my experience the day before in the garage. So I began the long process, utilizing my day off on Mondays and with my friend's advice, expertise and tools, I began the process of rebuilding each body part. A few weeks later I heard about an old business that was closing down, that had a number of forty-year-old parts still in a back room. I gladly took home a truck load of the priceless gems, for the bargain price of twenty-five dollars.

Soon I heard of a new business in town that specialized in parts for antique automobiles. People from all over the country ordered reproduction parts from this company, and God had placed this resource right in my back yard. Everything I needed was available.

In a little over two years, the pickup stood gleaming and complete. The beauty of the dark green body contrasting with the black fenders and running boards, was enhanced by the yellow spoke wheels. It was a showpiece and it was a glory to God. It was a project that wasn't only started, but was finished.

In my spirit I knew that God was pleased. I'm not implying that the restoration of an antique increases His kingdom, but through the power of the Holy Spirit, I followed through with a **vision** that had begun long ago. I knew that God was glorified.

THE GREATEST LACK IS LACK OF VISION

Without question, the church's greatest need is that of vision. Where there is no vision, people have nowhere to go and nothing to look forward to. The word, perish, in Proverbs 29:18 is the Hebrew word, para, which means to loosen, to unravel, or to be unrestrained. Without a vision, we move aimlessly and powerlessly without direction.

Satan's most vicious venom and strategic aim are not against the Christian's faith, but against his vision! Without a vision, he doesn't need faith. Faith always cooperates with vision. But without a vision, faith has nothing to cooperate with.

It is wonderful to be born-again, and have the power of the Holy Spirit in your life, but without a vision of God's purpose, you will not go far. Every Christian must seek God for His vision for his own life— both a long term and a short term vision. Also a vision is needed for the local church he is a part of. Without a vision of where your local church is going, you will be of little help to those people. One reason many churches do not grow is that the people do not share the vision of the pastor, or the pastor himself, does not have a vision. But the vision must be declared and made plain.

> "Then the Lord answered me and said: **'Write the vision and make it plain on tablets,** that he may run who reads it. For the vision is yet for an appointed time; But at the end it will speak, and it will not lie. Though it tarries, wait for it; because it will surely come, it will not tarry."
>
> Habakkuk 2:2-3

THE DEVIL THOUGHT UP SMALL THINKING

God is big. God thinks big. He does not know the meaning of small thinking. He is not limited by circumstances, nor by situations, and He certainly has no lack of resources. The only thing that limits God is man. God knows that nothing is impossible to visionaries, to those who dare to look beyond their present boundaries. But how easily we collapse into a small-thinking, poverty-stricken, limited mentality when there is no vision. In fact when men began to build a city with a tower whose top would be the heavens, He said,

> "Indeed the people are one and they all have one language, and this is what they begin to do; **now nothing that they purpose to do will be withheld from them.** Come, let Us go down and there confuse their language, that they may not understand one another's speech."
>
> Genesis 11:6-7

FAMILIAR ENEMIES

The longer I walk with God, the more obvious it becomes to me that the devil's onslaught is to remove vision out of people.

Feelings of unworthiness, hopelessness, inferiority, and insecurity are all part of hell's hindrances to suffocate our creative nature. Depression, heaviness and discouragement have often been diabolically assigned against those whom God's hand is mightily upon. I have to believe that the devil knows a portion of the awesomeness of God's plan for individual lives and the limitless potential He has put into the spirit of man. Therefore, to usurp years of that person's time by smothering and stifling his potential vision, continues to be the devil's strategy. But the Scripture says, "Let God arise and His enemies be scattered." Psalm 68:1 And David cries out,

> "To You, O Lord, I lift up my soul. O my God, I trust in You; Let me not be ashamed; Let not my enemies triumph over me."
>
> Psalm 25:1-2

Who are our enemies? They are old and familiar. Fear. Inferiority. Unworthiness. Discouragement.

Depression. Unbelief. Procrastination. Uselessness. The list goes on. The devil still uses old tactics. We already have authority over them through Jesus Christ. But **we** must shake them off. We must declare victory concerning our own lives. The victory is already ours, but we must rise up and take it.

One reason many do not overcome a weight problem, a drug problem, a lust problem, or even suicide tendencies is because of a lack of vision. If nothing fills that part of us that was meant to be filled with God's purpose, then all sort of negative persuasions have their say.

It is interesting that Paul the apostle, did not say, "Don't fulfill the lust of the flesh and you will walk (automatically) in the Spirit." It doesn't work that way, although much has been preached that implies that. But he said, "Walk in the Spirit, and you will not fulfill the lust of the flesh." Galatians 5:16

IF YOU GET EXCITED, GOD WILL GET EXCITED

As much as we hate to admit it, much of the time God is waiting upon us to possess the vision. If we will pursue it, He will pursue it with us. When I spoke to that mountain of antique truck parts in the garage, I meant what I said. Instantly, it was as if I could feel the excitement of the Holy Spirit within me. He wanted me to follow through with a task I had begun. And He was ready to follow through with me as soon as I made that decision.

There is something almost unrighteous about an uncompleted task. Can you picture heaven full of projects that God never got around to completing?

During a board meeting of the church I pastored,

one of the men who was a big thinker, suggested that the church ought to start a savings account. The thought had never occurred to me. In fact it seemed almost anti-God, as if it were a lack of faith or trust. Looking back, I see it differently. I see it as good stewardship. When this suggestion was made, my immediate reaction was that there was no money available to begin a savings account. Afterall, it was all we could do to meet our bills every month. But the man pursued his conviction, and therefore we started a savings account for the church with the same bank that was carrying our mortgage.

Almost immediately, extra money began to trickle in. There always seemed to be at least a hundred dollars or so each week to put aside. Before long it grew to over a thousand, until we were able to have a healthy reserve for emergencies, repairs of equipment, special needs, etc. There was no doubt that the Lord was pleased with this kind of stewardship. It was a vision.

When my daughter and son made the honor roll one year, I rewarded them by starting a savings account for each of them, putting some initial money in their account to give them a good start. Along with this, I made them a promise that whatever amount they would contribute to their accounts I would match that amount. At first they were excited and they would try to add something to their accounts every few days. Truthfully I was just as excited as they were about this vision of saving money. I was enthusiastic about matching every dollar amount that they put in.

As their father, I was devoted to their vision with them. But my participation was **limited** to their willingness to pursue the increase of their savings account. If they were willing, so was I. However, when they ceased to be excited, my hands were tied. Because according to our agreement, I could only match their deposit.

If we get excited about our vision, God will too! He will participate in it with us according to **our** willingness to pursue it. His faith will arise in us to match our vision to the extent that we seek it. If we don't embrace the vision, His hands are tied.

HAND TO MOUTH VISION

Many people never plan for the future. They live for the moment. They live from paycheck to paycheck, from payday to payday. Although this may be the norm for young -marrieds just starting out, eventually they need to institute a plan of action, a plan for the future. A savings account should be started, a financial plan for the children's college education, a retirement plan, etc.

Many Christians live from hand to mouth spiritually speaking. They have no concept of going anywhere, but living in a "just get by" mentality.

Rather than inquiring of God about His plan for their lives, they live only from Sunday to Sunday to acquire just enough spiritual food to get them to the next Sunday, and unfortunately a prayer life just to get them through one crisis until the next crisis comes. As the person who quickly spends his paycheck and lives in a crisis mentality until the next paycheck comes, they have no spiritual **life,** only an **existence.**

Sadly, the vision of many Christians ends with saying the sinner's prayer, claiming their right to eternal life insurance (assurance). Others carry their vision only on to the baptism of the Holy Spirit, with an occasional manifestation of a gift of the Holy Spirit in their lives.

But God is an ongoing God. It is never His

intention that we merely exist until Jesus comes, and our only life source being to savor past and remotely remembered experiences. His desire is for us to have abundant life daily. That can only come through a vision of His purpose and a vision to know Him intimately. We are people of destiny.

"I press toward the goal for the prize of the upward call of God in Christ Jesus."

Philippians 3:14

It is wise to state your vision outloud. Put it on the refrigerator, or on the dashboard of your car. As someone said, "If you don't know where you are going, how will you know when you get there?" Ask God to enlarge your vision. Ask Him to bring it into being. Keep it foremost in your thoughts, because it involves His kingdom. "Thy Kingdom come. Thy will be done."

SURROUND YOURSELF WITH BIG THINKERS

While preaching in a newly formed church, the Lord put a statement in my mouth. As I heard myself speak it, it amazed me. "It is hard to have a big vision when you are surrounded by small thinkers."

I love to be around people who think big. They provoke me. They challenge me. They stir me. One purpose of preaching is to stir us unto God in a larger way. As a preacher, I enjoy being around businessmen who have large visions. Hearing them talk of their latest venture and expressing their goals for their businesses, stirs me up to think more extravagantly spiritually.

Samuel commanded Saul, whom he had just anointed, to go stand among the prophets. The first thing we need to do is to get in the atmosphere of where the

Spirit is moving. Stop hanging around the complainers, and the gossips.

> "After that you shall come to the hill of God where the Philistine garrison is. And it will happen when you have come there to the city, that you will meet a group of prophets coming down from the high place with a stringed instrument, a tambourine, a flute, and a harp before them; and they will be prophesying. **Then the Spirit of the Lord will come upon you, and you will prophesy with them and be turned into another man."**
>
> I Samuel 10:5-6

God uses people to provoke our vision. Saul had never prophesied, yet when he came to the group of prophets he began prophesying. He turned into another man! When we are stirred and provoked, we tap into the potential that God has for us. We go past ourselves and beyond the path of limitation that we were on, and enter into a higher plane...a larger vision.

The Holy Spirit in each individual Christian has to be stirred up. That is why Paul boldly proclaimed to Timothy,

> "Therefore I remind you to stir up the gift of God **which is in you** through the laying on of my hands."
>
> II Timothy 1:6

Also we are exhorted to believe God according to the power that already works in us.

> "Now to Him who is able to do exceedingly abundantly above all that we ask or think, according to the **power that works in us.**"
>
> Ephesians 3:20

It is easy to believe that God has the power and that He can do exceedingly abundantly above all that we ask or think, but how quickly we ignore the fact that the Holy Spirit and His ability is in us. He is within us available to do exploits, but we must search out the vision He has for us.

SEE IT BEFORE YOU SEE IT!

We've known a number of people who have had a house built. But before the house is built, before a foundation is dug or any land is cleared, the home is a reality in their minds. They have a vision of the house and it is already in existence to them. They are more than willing to drive you by the property and tell you detail after detail of the design of the house, the style of kitchen and family room, the location of the bedrooms, and so forth.

Yet, if you look with your eyes, you see nothing but a bare piece of land. But to them it already exists. The fact that months of work and skilled laborers and materials are required, is irrelevant to them. They have a new house! It is a reality. They have a vision. The vision is substance. The house already exists in their minds.

When God spoke to Joshua concerning Jericho, the first sentence He said to Joshua was "See!" Joshua first had to simply **see** Jericho as already defeated. He couldn't see a walled and mammoth city. He had to see a defeated Jericho.

> "See! I **have given** Jericho into your hand, its king, and the mighty men of valor."
>
> Joshua 6:2

God didn't tell Joshua that He was **going** to give him the city. He told him that He **had already given it to him.** Therefore He commanded Joshua to first see! Once Joshua saw Jericho defeated, then he was able to walk out each step of obedience with confidence. Had he not seen it as already done, he would not have had the courage to obey.

Many times we are robbed of what God has for us because we refuse to see as God sees. God always talks as if it already exists. Jesus called Peter a rock, while we would have observed him as anything but a rock. But God believes what He says **already** exists.

> " '...You are Simon the son of Jonah. You shall be called Cephas.' (which is translated, A stone)."
>
> John 1:42

Jesus was simply prophesying to Peter. This word of prophecy to Peter was calling forth the nature of Christ within Him. The Holy Spirit moves the same way today in our lives. He calls forth the potential of what He wants us to be and how He desires to use us.

Peter's future actions were irrelevant to Jesus because He believed what He had prophesied concerning Peter. Finally, it was Peter, who on the day of Pentecost, laid his life on the line and proclaimed to a crowd of potential executioners,

> "Therefore let all the house of Israel know assuredly that God has made this Jesus, whom you crucified, both Lord and Christ."
>
> Acts 2:36

The angel of the Lord appeared to Gideon and said,

> "The Lord is with you, you mighty man of valor!"
>
> Judges 6:12

Then God, knowing what He said was already so, said to Gideon,

> "Go in this **might of yours**, and you shall save Israel from the hand of the Midianites. Have I not sent you?"
>
> (vs. 14)

Everything God says, as far as He is concerned, already exists. It is a present reality. It was irrelevant whether Gideon felt like a mighty warrior. He probably felt more like a chicken. But God cannot lie.

God is the Creator. He continually calls into existence things that do not appear to exist. (Romans 4:17) Therefore we must see as God sees. We must "see" ourselves victorious before we will indeed see ourselves victorious.

As individuals we must see ourselves as God sees us. We are His own righteousness; we are more than conquerors; we are overcomers; victorious and mighty in God. We are His inheritance!

When I first purchased that old dilapidated truck, it was new to me. I owned it. The fact that it was a pile of junk (I only paid $50.00 for it) was irrelevant to me. I **saw** it as complete and restored.

When God saves us, we are His property, purchased with the price of His own blood. We are new creations. He doesn't see the work that needs to be done. He sees the completed product. He has a vision concerning us! He is going to strip off everything that hides the image of Himself within us. While we were yet sinners He died for us, and saw us washed in His blood and serving Him. Jesus was the Lamb slain **before** the foundation of the world. We are His vision!

RESOURCES GRAVITATE TO VISION

We made a decision to pay our church off five years after we made the original loan. At that time, we still owed almost as much toward the balance, as we did at the inception of the loan.

The vision to pay it off was exciting. However, we had no extra resources to pay it off. At the end of every month, when all the bills were paid, there was very little left over. Our natural minds reasoned to wait until we had a surplus of money before attempting to pay extra increments on the mortgage balance.

But surpluses and resources don't just arrive, they gravitate to the vision!

Therefore, when we brought the vision before the people, we were not concerned where the money would come from. Our main motive and concern was that God had indeed spoken that we were to pay it off. That is when it became exciting, and many began to embrace the vision with us. Whatever extra we had, even if it was only fifty dollars, we applied it weekly to the balance. Each week the amount would increase! THE VISION WAS CALLING FORTH THE INCREASE!

Had we not embraced the vision, the money would not have come forth. Faith arose to the level of our vision. God became excited when we became excited.

In fact a month or so after we began to put extra money toward the mortgage, a check for several thousand dollars came from a most unlikely source. A college student, who could barely afford meals, was moved on to help toward the building fund. He explained how he had received a large financial settlement over an accident that he had been in several years before. He gave a tithe of his settlement. I believe the vision to pay the church off called forth the settlement of the lawsuit. Resources gravitate to vision.

So often we are concerned with resources rather than vision. If we embrace the vision, God will take care of the resources. We must look to God's ability, rather than to our inability.

The emphasis should not be upon faith, because faith will quickly rise to the level of our vision. Like many, I have gotten in strife trying to work up my faith, but that is the hard way. Once you see the vision of what God is calling you to do, your faith will concur with the vision. Your faith is always equal to the level of your vision.

When a seed is planted in the ground, everything begins to gravitate to it. The soil gives the nutrients that it needs The sun and the rain gravitate to its needs. Whatever the seed needs will be manifested to it. But someone has to have the vision of planting the seed. Nothing will gravitate to it until it is planted.

This is equally true with vision. When we plant the seed of our vision into God, whatever resources it needs will manifest. Without the vision, no resources are needed. Without a vision, we move aimlessly and haphazardly. "Without a vision the people perish." Proverbs 29:18

MOVING IN GOD PREVENTS SPIRITUAL PARALYSIS

God has called us to be visionaries. Not only are lost people without Christ, they are also without vision. We have been made in God's image and He is a creator and He is a visionary.

No wonder the devil would try to suppress our creative nature and destroy lives by manipulating young people into suicide or burning their brains with drugs.

Every person needs vision. We need not only to be saved from sin and filled with the Holy Spirit, we need to possess the vision of what God has called us to be.

Many sincere Christian people sit in churches paralyzed because they have no vision. They have been taught that the ultimate is to receive salvation or to be healed or to speak in tongues. But the ultimate is to flow into the purpose of God for our lives. And only He can reveal it. That is why we must seek Him for the vision.

The vision contains the potential fruit. It is fruit that will remain.

You don't need faith, you need vision!

4

Encourage Yourself!

—You cannot encourage someone else, if you're
not encouraged yourself.

"...But David strengthened himself in the Lord his God."
I Samuel 30:6

It was Monday morning. Feeling that I had let God down in a situation the previous day, and convinced that I blew an opportunity to let God use me as He could have, I found a secluded spot and began to pray. Because I was so upset at myself, my prayer was a rash outpouring of my frustration to God. I informed Him what a failure I was and questioned His judgment of using me at all. As I continued this tirade of condemnation of myself, the Holy Spirit suddenly spoke to my spirit three words. "Stop riveting yourself." His voice was a firm command. I was not to pray that way any longer, God had no interest in hearing the summation of my weaknesses and failings. I was grieving the Holy Spirit.

As I sat there musing upon what the Holy Spirit had said, I began to see the reality of what He was saying. Prayer is not unloading our misery on God. Prayer is communication. It is a two-way conversation. When I carry on this one-sided plastering of accusations against myself (His creation), the Lord can rightly say, "You're not making My day" or "I'm not getting a lot out of this." In fact when we use prayer as a vehicle to unload our "garbage" on God about our lack, our problems, our failings, our resentments, and then proclaim that we feel better having prayed, God might well reply, **"I don't."**

45

Rather than pray from our vantage point, which may well be distorted because of our inability to see the overall picture, we must pray from His perspective, which agrees with His word. Rather than praying our lack, we can pray acknowledging God's abundance; His ability, not our inability; His resources, rather than our lack of resources.

Proclaiming oneself as a failure, only declares Him the king of a failure. Obviously such a statement doesn't glorify God. You may fail, but you are not a failure. You are God's own righteousness, but not by anything you have done, only by His grace.

No husband is encouraged to hear his wife call herself ugly or undesirable. That only makes him consider that he is married to such a one. Likewise, a wife doesn't get joy out of her husband's complaining that he's a failure. That only makes her the wife of a failure. God gets no glory when we refuse to see ourselves as He sees us.

DON'T BEAT UP ON YOURSELF!

God's people have a bad habit of beating up on themselves. I'm glad Jesus didn't say to Peter, "Beat My sheep," but rather "Feed My sheep." (John 21)

No one would want to go to a doctor who didn't have confidence in his own ability. How ridiculous it would be while waiting for the surgeon to prepare to operate on you, to hear him mumble, "I should have been a mechanic." Or "Everyone I operate on seems to die." This would only make you want to find the closest and quickest exit. Yet we downgrade ourselves continually, thinking it is humility. Humility has nothing to do with poor self-esteem. That is false humility.

Christians have prayed so long, "Lord, I'm not worthy," that we think we are being humble. But the truth is, He has made us worthy. We are worthy to receive all that He has for us, but not because of anything **we** have done, but because we have been brought into covenant with Him, through His own blood. The best surgeon in the world would rightly be humble if he stated, "I am an excellent surgeon, because God has given me the ability."

When the devil attempts to get you to beat up on yourself, just say, "I'm God's own righteousness and I'm worthy to receive, but I didn't get here on my own. And the same God who put me here by His grace, is big enough to keep me standing here in His grace."

YOU CAN'T HEAR FROM GOD IF YOU'RE DISCOURAGED

Discouraged people don't hear from God. You cannot hear from God if you feel like a failure. Thank God for the Holy Spirit. He is the Encourager. Jesus called Him the Paraclete, or the Helper. He helps us stay encouraged and in communion with God. Without faith it is impossible to please God (Hebrews 11:6), but we cannot move in faith if we don't have fellowship and communion with God. He speaks to expectant hearts, and so it is difficult to hear Him if we are continually discouraged and under condemnation.

I believe that one of the devil's most frequently used weapons against the saints is discouragement. He knows discouraged or distracted hearts will hinder both our communion with God and our hearing His voice and thus responding in obedience to Him. That is why I refuse to surround myself with negative people. (That is unless they desire to change).

Some enjoy being negative and feel better pulling others down with them. I call them the "cold-water ministries." No matter what you are excited about, they somehow are able to throw cold water on it. They can find a problem in every opportunity. I don't need it! I don't have time to feel discouraged.

Since it is impossible to please God without faith, I cannot give into discouragement and listen to the discouragers. I have to stay encouraged so I can hear from God, and as a result, move in faith. No wonder God told Joshua to "Be strong and of good courage." (Joshua 1:6,7,9) To discourage is to take the courage out of you.

I believe in encouragement. Encouraged people soon hear from God. An encouraged heart is a heart open to hear the Holy Spirit. Some have made a decision to remain discouraged, but most only need a little encouragement, like a little water to a wilting plant. Soon that one will thrive again.

ENCOURAGE ONE ANOTHER

We need to encourage one another in the Lord.

"Therefore comfort and edify (encourage) one another, just as you also are doing."

I Thessalonians 5:11

Encouragement causes hope, but discouragement brings hopelessness and despair. Encouraged people begin to expect good things from God, and expectation is the key to seeing the miraculous power of God. We must guard against anything that destroys our sense of expectation of the goodness of God. This includes harsh and condemnatory preaching of the gospel. David said, "I would have lost heart (fainted), unless I had believed that I would see the goodness of the Lord in the land of the living." Psalm 27:13

David lived with a sense of expectation from God. He purposed to be a man after God's heart. (Acts 13:22) When he found himself in a devastating circumstance at Ziklag, he knew how to touch the heart of God. The Amalekites had attacked Ziklag and burned it with fire, and had taken captive their wives, and their sons and daughters.

> "Then David was greatly distressed, for the people spoke of stoning him, because the soul of all the people was grieved, every man for his sons and daughters. But David **strengthened himself** in the Lord his God."
>
> I Samuel 30:6

It was at such a point that David could have harshly condemned himself and cried out "Failure!" and conceded defeat, saying, "I missed God somewhere." But David knew about the goodness of God and dared to look past his predicament. He possessed an understanding of God's greatness that far superseded the situation confronting him.

However, **before** David could hear God, he had to first encourage himself in the Lord. He knew He could not hear from God in a devastated mentality, so he shook off the discouragement and dared to believe that God would turn this calamity into good.

The first step to hearing from God is always to encourage yourself. When your heart is encouraged it is conditioned to receive good news. For example, when a small child is crying over a broken toy, the mother first has to calm the child down and get him to stop crying, before she can tell him she is going to buy him a new one. It is hard to hear good news when our hearts are in anguish. When Moses prophesied good news to the children of Israel that God was going to bring them out

49

from under the burdens of the Egyptians, they could **not hear** the good news. Their spirits were in anguish.

"So Moses spoke thus to the children of Israel; but they would not heed Moses, **because of anguish of spirit and cruel bondage."**

Exodus 6:9

Then David prayed with confidence and expectation to the Lord.

"So David inquired of the Lord, saying, 'Shall I pursue this troop? Shall I overtake them?' And He answered him, 'Pursue, for you shall surely overtake them and without fail recover all.' "

(vs. 8)

What an awesome word from God! Yet David would have never heard that directive from God if he had chosen to remain in that discouraged state.

Discouragement is a decision. We have to make a conscious decision to be discouraged. Contrary to popular belief, no one can discourage you! You must make a conscious decision to be discouraged on your own volition! But you can also make a decision not to give into discouragement. When the decision is made to encourage yourself in the Lord, your heart is geared to hear good news from the Lord.

DON'T WAIT FOR SOMEONE TO ENCOURAGE YOU

David didn't wait for someone to encourage him. He encouraged **himself;** not in circumstances, but in the Lord. There may not always be someone around to encourage you, but you can encourage yourself. Begin to render thanksgiving unto God. Tell Him that you appreciate His blessings and faithfulness. A thankful heart is a precedence for good mental health. Many are so self-centered and wrapped up in their own lives (I speak of

Christians) that they are not aware that you need encouragement. So don't wait for someone to tell you good news, just go to God. "God is our refuge and strength, **a very present help** in trouble." Psalm 46:1 If you get strengthened in God, you will automatically be a strength to others which will spawn much encouragement. No wonder Paul said concerning the manifestation of the gifts of the Holy Spirit, "...Let all things be done for edification." I Corinthians 14:26 The most unselfish thing you can do is desire that the gifts of the Holy Spirit work in you so that through you, others will be edified.

> "But he who prophesies speaks edification, and exhortation and comfort to men."
>
> I Corinthians 14:3

Of course, the devil will try to stop you from yielding to the Holy Spirit. He has one reason, to keep the body of Christ from being edified and encouraged! Therefore cast down those thoughts that you're showing off, or thoughts that God doesn't want to use you. Who does God use? He uses those who will yield to the Holy Spirit.

JOY IS NORMAL CHRISTIAN LIVING

If we learn to live in the presence of God, we are going to hear Him issuing commands. That is why it is **normal** to be encouraged and full of expectation. Those feelings are not meant solely for times of revival or conventions. It is meant to be a normal part of life. It should be normal for the born-again, blood-washed Christian to be full of joy.

Sadly, when a brand new Christian is experiencing the joy of the Lord for the first time and is full of zeal for God, a well-meaning "mature" Christian comes along with words such as "This won't last, because God is going to test your faith," or "Be on guard, the devil is going to attack you." Why do we lay such gloom and doom on those young in the Lord? That new Christian is just experiencing normal Christian living. His expectancy and faith toward God are high.

Yes, he will grow and will experience opposition from the devil and have to overcome many obstacles in His Christian walk, and may well suffer persecution. **But he need not lose His sense of joyful expectation!** As marriage was meant to proceed and grow beyond the honeymoon, so it is in our walk with God. Truthfully we should say, "If you think it is wonderful now, just wait, because life with Jesus gets better and better."

If we have been robbed of our joy and think we are being spiritual by "holding on," we have forgotten that Jesus promised us abundant life. Yes, there will be obstacles and hindrances, and even trials, but He promised He would never leave or forsake us. "...In the world you will have tribulation; but be of good cheer, I have overcome the world." John 16:33

Think of the glory that God received as David came marching back with all the wives, sons and daughters, and their possessions!

> "So David recovered all that the Amalekites had carried away, and David rescued his two wives. And nothing of theirs was lacking, either small or great, sons or daughters, spoil or anything which they had taken from them; David recovered all."
>
> (vs. 18-19)

ENCOURAGED PEOPLE HEAR FROM GOD

The very nature of the Holy Spirit is to encourage. He is the Comforter, the Helper, the Teacher. When Jesus cast a legion of demons out of a totally possessed man, the man begged Him that he might be with Him continually. But Jesus said to him,

> "Go home to your friends, and tell them what great things the Lord has done for you, and how He has had compassion on you."
>
> Mark 5:19

God wanted the message out. He wanted to use the man to spread encouragement to his friends, so they could know about God's compassion. Imagine how much faith was stirred up in those who heard! Imagine their encouragement, after the devil had convinced them God didn't care about the needs of people. No doubt from this encouraging report, they too began to believe God for greater things. The Holy Spirit instills hope, and when people begin to hope, they begin to **hear** from God.

It is so vital for each of us to ask the Lord to manifest Himself to us daily. When He manifests a miracle for you, it has a ripple effect, as when a rock is thrown into a pool of water. Many lives are going to be touched by your miracle. That is why I believe in the importance of living with expectation. It "pulls" the miraculous power out of God. It is not a problem of His touching you, but your touching Him!

> "...And as many as **touched Him** were made well."
>
> Mark 6:56

It is not God's decision how many miracles happen in our lives or in specific worship services. God is always willing to do awesome things. But we set our sights too low. We settle for religious doldrums, when we could see the Lord move in might and power. He will, if we yield to Him; if we listen for His voice; if we live with expectation.

It is unselfish to expect God to do a miracle for you, even if it is the healing of a wart! Your miracle will provoke and induce others to believe. Never have an attitude "Well, I don't need anything." Ask God to do something for you that will splash on to others. As someone said, "If brother cup overflows, brother saucer will get blessed."

Some sit around thinking, "Well, I want to see a crippled person healed." But God may well rebuke them for not believing for even the small miracles. You can't have "wheelchair faith" if you don't have faith for a skin condition. You have to start somewhere. Stir up your faith!

DISTORTED EXPECTATIONS

When the king of Moab rebelled against King Jehoram of Israel, Jehoram requested help from Jehoshaphat, King of Judah. When he and Jehoshaphat and the king of Edom found themselves desperate for water for the army and the animals, the king of Israel lost hope.

> "And the king of Israel said, 'Alas! For the Lord has called these three kings together to deliver them into the hand of Moab.'"
>
> II Kings 3:10

What a negative report! What an accusation against God! As some do, the moment something looks discouraging, they begin to accuse God of bringing destruction upon them. Although they were on the verge of a miracle, all the king of Israel could do was accuse God of wanting to destroy them. What a distorted perspective of an awesome God!

But thank God for Jehoshaphat. He encouraged himself in the Lord.

> "**But** Jehoshaphat said, 'Is there no prophet of the Lord here, that we may inquire of the Lord by him?' And one of the servants of the king of Israel answered and said, 'Elisha the

son of Shaphat is here, who poured water on the hands of Elijah.'"

(vs. 11)

When they found the prophet Elisha, the prophetic word of the Lord came through him,

"But now bring me a musician." And it happened, when the musician played that the hand of the Lord came upon him. And he said, 'Thus says the Lord, **"Make this valley full of ditches."'** For thus says the Lord: 'You shall not see rain; yet that valley shall be filled with water, so that you, your cattle, and your animals may drink.' And this is but a trivial thing in the sight of the Lord; He will also deliver the Moabites into your hand."

(vs. 15-16)

They were commanded to dig ditches; ditches of faith; ditches of expectation! God would fill the ditches with water but not according to anything that would agree with the natural and reasoning senses. He would do it by His power.

If He had done it by rain, the enemy would have recognized that the ditches were full of water. But since God filled them miraculously, the enemy saw the sun shining on the water and discerned it to be blood. Then they assumed that the kings had fought and killed one another. When they ran to the camp of Israel thinking they would plunder the spoil, Israel rose up and attacked them, killing them.

"So when they came to the camp of Israel, Israel rose up and attacked the Moabites, so they fled before them; and they entered their land, killing the Moabites."

(vs. 25)

VICTORY!

The bottom line is God wants every Christian to walk in victory. God is glorified through victory. We must choose to be open to His voice, His wisdom and His Spirit every moment. It is His will that we are encouraged and are an encouragement to others.

In every area of our lives where we let the Lord work with us, whether it means admitting mistakes, or successes of hearing His voice, we will **automatically** minister to others in those areas of life.

It is not just what we say that ministers to people, but who we are. And we become like Him as we let Him manifest Himself to us and in us. For example, if you surrender your depression to God, and let Him minister His joy in its place, you will always minister joy to others. This will occur even when you are not conscious of it, because it is His joy manifesting in you. You have become a partaker of the Divine nature!

5

Principles of Hearing From God

—When you begin to hear from God, you begin to grow.

"None of them shall teach his neighbor, and none his brother, saying,'Know the Lord,' **for all shall know Me**, from the least of them to the greatest of them."   Hebrews 8:11

What has stunted the growth of Christians more than anything else is the lack of teaching that every Christian can and should know how to hear the voice of God.

It is normal for every Christian to hear from God. Jesus said, "My sheep hear My voice, and I know them, and they follow Me." John 10:27

Much teaching implies that no one really hears from God until he gets to heaven, or that only a few "spiritual giants" hear from God. But nothing could be further from the truth. God wants us to experience daily communication with Him. In fact, it is abnormal **not** to hear the voice of the Lord.

The good news of the new covenant is "All shall know Me, from the least of them to the greatest of them." Hebrews 8:11

GOD DOESN'T TALK TO YOUR BRAIN, BUT TO YOUR SPIRIT

The human mind is often like a five-mile flea market, or as a radio turned on full-blast, blaring all day long. The mind is every Christian's problem. It is the loud, reasoning, analytical, scrutinizing mind that is our enemy when it comes to hearing from the Holy Spirit.

"Because the carnal (natural, fleshly) mind is enmity (hostile, contrary) against God; for it is not subject to the law of God, nor indeed can be."

Romans 8:7

The devil is not our problem as much as our brain is our problem. It is not the voice of the Lord that is intermittent, but our hearing that is intermittent.

Much misunderstanding comes from the question of where we hear from God, not how. We hear from God in our inner man. Deep in the core of our being, in our spirit, is where we will hear the Lord. As we grow, we become more sensitive to Him. Although His voice does not grow louder, we learn to command our souls (minds and emotions) to be still so we can recognize His voice. He abides within every Christian. He is faithful every day, twenty-four hours a day.

"But the anointing which you have received from Him abides in you, and you do not need that anyone teach you; but as the same anointing teaches you concerning **all things**, and is true, and is not a lie, and just as it has taught you, you will abide in Him."

I John 2:27

The Holy Spirit within us will guide us into all truth and will teach us continually the difference between the truth and a lie. He cannot be fooled, and if we listen to Him, neither will we!

The problem with the church is that we have grown in information and not in hearing and knowing God.

Normal Christian living is to know the voice of the Lord in our own spirit. Normal Christian growth is becoming more sensitive to His voice, as a result of walking in obedience to what we hear Him say.

LET GOD CONTROL YOUR HEART

Many Christians hear from God and don't know it. The main reason is we make it too complicated by believing that we somehow live separate from Him. He abides. He lives within us every moment of every day.

When Elijah stood before King Ahab, he knew he was also standing in the presence of the Lord. He had no sense of being separated from God's presence. He declared,

> "As the Lord God of Israel lives, **before whom I stand**, there shall not be dew nor rain these years, except at **my word**."
>
> I Kings 17:1

Peter understood what it meant to abide in the presence of the living God when he declared to the crippled man at the gate Beautiful, **"What I do have I give to you."** (Acts 3)

God speaks from within. He has set up His authority and kingship in the center of our being. The problem is not getting Him to speak, but rather to recognize that He is speaking.

For example, when I was a pastor in Beaumont, Texas, frequently we would have people stop by the church for help. The majority simply wanted food, or gas or money. Most of them were transients whose life style consisted of an aimless path down America's highways, usually appealing for free handouts. Others were hard-luck cases—out of work, a car broken down, robbed, or out of gas.

Since our church was right along Interstate 10 we acquired a rather unusual amount of such requests for help.

It was through some of these incidents that I learned how God controls the heart. Sometimes I would look into the sun- aged face of a seemingly sincere wanderer and feel a rush of sympathy for him, and even guilt that I was so much better off. Yet in that moment as he would ask me for his hand-out I would sense my heart becoming hard and calloused toward him. Usually I would obey what I felt and turn him away. But later I would condemn and accuse myself for being so cruel and cold-hearted. But God knew what He was talking about. He would not have me giving kingdom money to fulfill vices such as alcohol and drugs, rather than legitimate needs.

At other times someone would come who didn't appear to me to have a sincere need. However, as I would hear the familiar story of hard-luck, suddenly deep in my inner man I would feel a surge of compassion. Usually I would obey this prompting and give him the help he wanted. Obviously God wanted to minister to him, as He looks upon the heart and not the outward appearance. But later I would again chide myself for being too spineless and soft-hearted.

However, the Holy Spirit was teaching me valuable lessons. He was ruling within my heart. As I would take heed to what I felt in my insides, those feelings proved to be accurate. It was the Holy Spirit within me who was hardening my heart and softening my heart toward needs. My job was to pay attention to Him. However, as most people do, I would condemn myself for these feelings.

God is smarter than we are! It takes us to realize that. He knows the hearts of people. He has access to facts that we do not have. Therefore our responsibility is to obey what He tells our inner man.

TRUST YOUR INNER MAN

What we sense in our inner man often contradicts what we feel with our natural reasoning. But the Holy Spirit within us can be depended upon. We should let Him control our hearts! His expertise is in management. Our expertise is in obedience.

Many hear from God and instantaneously suppress that knowledge or feeling because it is contrary to the status quo of the people they are around. For example, when the Holy Spirit is quenched by a song leader, most know it instantly. However, not wanting to believe it, they brush it off as a critical spirit trying to get a foot in the door and go on, blaming themselves for being so "unspiritual." For months or even years they may place blame on themselves, criticizing their inability to recognize the presence of God. But in reality, they were hearing God all along. The Holy Spirit in our inner man never lies.

Of course, we are to cover people in love, as when a song leader quenches the Spirit. But that doesn't mean we are to pretend there is not a problem. True spirituality means we will recognize and discern things. Why? Our inner man is growing.

> "But he who is spiritual judges (appraises) all things, yet he himself is judged by no one."
>
> I Corinthians 2:15

True spirituality also means that we are discreet with what God reveals to us. The more God opens our eyes to things, the more we must give ourselves to pray about them. Love covers a multitude of sins. We must have wisdom not to disclose weaknesses, but to always go to the source of the problem in love.

But the bottom line is that it is possible and normal

to hear from God and that we can tune into what He is saying.

STRENGTHENING THE INNER MAN

In Christian circles, we often hear so much about what is going on in a certain city where there is a great church or a successful ministry, that we are led to believe that is where the ultimate presence of God is. But the issue is not that God is in a certain place, but that He is within the individual Christian!

We hear too much about places and people. We need to know that Christ is manifesting Himself to each individual person. "All shall know Me..." Be thankful that He is moving in certain places and using certain people, but be excited that He is moving in you!

God is always concerned about the condition of our inner man. That is the real person.

> "That He would grant you, according to the riches of His glory, to be strengthened with might through His Spirit **in the inner man.**"
>
> Ephesians 3:16

It is through the strength of our inner man that we overcome discouragement, depression and defeat. It is through the inner man that we rise above all attacks and hindrances of the enemy. It is through the strength of our inner man that we defeat the devil. It is through our inner man that we stir up faith, hear from God, and have communication and fellowship with Him.

We are spirit beings. We live in a bodies, and we possess souls. Our spirits are to rule as kings, our souls as servants, and our bodies as slaves.

In the world the emphasis is on the body. The

fitness of the body occupies books, billboards and television commercials. The spirit receives no attention. But in God, things are right-side up. Our spirits are in command. It is our spirits that receive direction from God and tell our souls (as servants) how to act, and our bodies (as slaves) to subject to discipline.

Therefore the Holy Spirit is available to help us to be strong in our inner man. God knows that when our inner man is strong and victorious that we will be victorious. When we have joy within, our outlook on everything else becomes healthy. When we have peace within, circumstances are irrelevant, because our inner man is in charge.

Most of the prophetic utterance that comes to people, is God speaking to the inner man. The Holy Spirit is encouraging the inner man to walk in the fulfillment of God's total victory and purpose.

"But he who prophesies speaks edification and exhortation and comfort to men."

I Corinthians 14:4

Although prophecy also gives specific confirmation of direction to individuals, the primary purpose is to edify, exhort and comfort. A friend of mine put it this way: Edify, to build up; exhort, to stir up; and comfort, to cheer up.

DEVELOPING THE INNER MAN (MUSCLES OR MUSH?)

The inner man can be compared to a muscle. It is strengthened and developed by use. Our inner man has ears and eyes just like our physical body has ears and eyes. We have two sets!

Every great Christian leader's downfall comes when

he ceases to take heed to listen to the voice of the Holy Spirit in the inner man. It is easy to become too busy or over- confident, or to let an inflated ego callous that inner ear.

Most would consider it foolish to go to a doctor and request stronger muscles. He would simply say to go out and exercise consistently. No matter how much money you would be willing to pay your doctor, he still couldn't help you. He cannot give you stronger muscles. That comes by your exercise alone. There is no other way.

Yet when we go to God, we complain because we cannot hear Him. But God simply tells us to exercise our inner man. Our ability to hear God increases with exercising our spirits in listening to Him. That is why the Bible declares that many are dull of hearing. (Hebrews 5:11-14)

STEPS IN HEARING GOD

STEP #1 APPROACH GOD AS YOUR FRIEND

It is of utmost significance to talk to God as if He is your best friend. By the way, He is! Therefore you can approach Him with confidence, shaking off all feelings of guilt and inadequacy. Many fear a judgment from God or a nitpicking, but all wrath was poured out on His Son. He will not be upset or resentful if you come to Him as a son asking for wisdom.

> "If any of you lacks wisdom, let him ask of God, who **gives liberally and without reproach**, and it will be given to him."
>
> James 1:5

STEP #2 REMEMBER THAT HE IS NOT GOING TO GIVE YOU SOMETHING EVIL.

Be convinced that God is not going to hand you anything evil. He has your best interest in mind.

"Every good gift and every perfect gift is from above, and comes down from the Father of lights, with whom there is **no variation or shadow of turning.**"

James 1:17

"If you then, being evil, know how to give good gifts to your children, how much more will your heavenly Father give the Holy Spirit to those who ask Him!"

Luke 11:13

STEP #3 ASK EXPECTING TO RECEIVE AN ANSWER

God is more than willing to give wisdom to us and talk to us concerning most anything, whether it concerns natural decisions or spiritual decisions. But in the moment we are praying for direction, we must actively expect an answer. He will often speak in that very moment. God commands that if we are asking Him, we must be convinced that He is willing to tell us the answer.

"If any of you lacks wisdom, let him ask of God, who gives to **all liberally and without reproach**, and it will be given to him. But let him ask in faith, with no doubting, for he who doubts is like a wave of the sea driven and tossed by the wind. For let not that man suppose that he will receive anything from the Lord; he is a double-minded man, unstable in all his ways."

James 1:5-8

STEP #4 DON'T BE BOUND TO SOMETHING SENSATIONAL

Many equate anything to do with God as having to be big and loud and sensational. But rarely does God speak in a sensational manner. His voice quietly communes with our inner man.

Elijah did not hear God in the fire, the earthquake or the wind, but He did hear Him in the still small voice. (I Kings 17)

Power is noiseless! Electrical power has no noise.

Dynamite has no noise. There is no noise in the kitchen until an appliance is plugged into the outlet. Then the noise comes from the appliance, not from the power source. Dynamite has no noise, but the mountain blown to bits has noise.

Many have mistakenly equated God with noise and thus have missed His still small voice. It takes no faith to listen to noise, but it takes faith to listen for the still small voice of the Holy Spirit. For preachers, it is not the volume of the voice, but the depth of the anointing.

When God speaks the same word of power to two different people, one may just quietly smile, the other may give out a heart-stopping "Hallelujah," but the power is the same. Only the reaction varies. The question is not how dramatic your reaction is, but whether you embraced the word of the Lord that God spoke.

STEP #5 DON'T BE AFRAID OF MISSING GOD

A common misconception is the inference that whatever you do, don't miss God. But we are free to miss God. No one hears from God perfectly, and the only way to improve on our ability to hear God is by simply taking the risk of acting upon what we hear. We cannot hear God clearly if we continually live in fear of missing Him. In fact some try so hard not to miss God, that they miss him in the trying.

Although in the body of Christ we have not accorded one another the luxury of making mistakes, we are indeed free to make them. But truly mistakes are only meant to be a part of the training process. There is nothing wrong with making mistakes in endeavoring to hear God, as long as we are willing to admit and take responsibility for times when we thought we heard God and it became obvious we didn't.

The only thing we are at a risk to lose is pride.

STEP #6 KNOW THAT THE HOLY SPIRIT WILL OFTEN CONTRADICT YOUR NATURAL REASONING!

God is smarter than you are! He knows the end of a situation from the beginning. He is the Alpha and the Omega, the Beginning and the End. So many times when we pray for direction, we are surprised at what the Holy Spirit tells us. It is contrary to what our own common sense would have concluded. But as we obeyed (and sometimes didn't) we would find out that He knew what He was talking about all along. Obviously He has access to information that we don't have. It sure makes us appreciate the Holy Spirit.

STEP #7 REALIZE THAT GOD IS PRACTICAL

Sometimes we do not recognize what God is saying to us because we are trying to be too spiritual.

The most practical thing to do when asking the Lord for direction is to **be specific!**

Always go to the Lord with one question at a time. Then wait upon Him for a few moments to speak to you concerning that question. Usually in those few seconds or minutes He will speak to your spirit very gently, but very keenly by showing you a picture which would describe the answer, or a tremendous peace (or lack of peace if the answer is no) concerning the specific thing you are praying about, or even an instant knowledge in your spirit.

After you are clear about what He has spoken to you, then go on to another question. It often helps to write down what came to you at that moment, as things that come by the Holy Spirit are usually easily forgotten. The reason we so quickly forget what He says is simple: Anything that comes from the Spirit is not a product of the reasoning, natural mind. He talks directly to our spirit, bypassing all intellectual processes. Therefore the mind has trouble retaining it.

Also it helps to pray with someone who is willing to listen to the Lord with you. It must be someone who is willing to yield to a holy hush (not spooky), giving the Spirit an opportunity to speak clearly, and a person who is willing to submit his analytical reasoning mind to the Holy Spirit. After a few moments of prayer about a specific subject, you might share with one another what the Lord revealed to you regarding what you were asking Him about.

When my wife and I sit down and pray specifically about decisions we need to make, the majority of the time we receive the same answer from the Lord. We have found that the greatest obstacle is getting our minds and emotions out of the way.

STEP #8 FAST FROM YOUR THOUGHTS

Jesus lived on a perpetual fast from His thoughts. He lived a life of choosing to listen to the voice of the Father. (John 5:30; John 8:28-29)

We too can fast from our thoughts and opinions. If we have our own opinion and make a quick judgment on everything, there is no room to hear God.

You are most available to hear God when you don't have an opinion. Sadly, our minds are frequently so cluttered with input from everything but the Spirit of God, that we have left no room for Him to speak. We must return to that childlike innocence and purity of heart. No wonder Paul warned against the vanity of the mind by saying,

> "But I fear, lest somehow, as the serpent deceived Eve by his craftiness, so your minds may be corrupted from the simplicity that is in Christ."
>
> II Corinthians 11:3

Keep it simple.

STEP #9 DON'T GET SPOOKY

I always get concerned when some people get so mystical when you talk about hearing the voice of the Lord. God is extremely practical, and desires to give us wisdom. It is possible to live a normal life, to look normal and act normal and still just hear from God and live with supernatural wisdom and power. Be on guard against all religious theatrics. God isn't impressed. Besides, you will scare away the very people you want to help, no matter how sincere you are.

GROWTH COMES BY HEARING

There is little spiritual growth until the Christian begins to exercise his or her own spirit. Hearing of and admiring the experiences of others, may challenge you, but will only help you to the extent their testimony provokes you to seek God for your own experiences. Testimonies are like samples to provoke your desire. Just as in a supermarket, often there will be people stationed in the store offering sample tidbits of delicious food. These will not serve as a meal, as their purpose is to make you want to buy a larger quantity. You cannot get fat on samples!

Spiritual growth comes by having your own experiences! Response and obedience to the Holy Spirit cause the spiritual man to exercise and thus grow. But there is no way to respond to God if you are not hearing from God.

A minister will do you a favor if he challenges you to hear from God for yourself. Rather than spout off a pat answer, you would be far more helped by a challenge such as "What is the Father telling you? What are you hearing about this situation in your own spirit?" As you begin to hear God, you will experience immediate growing and stretching in your own spirit.

This is not to say that anyone is to develop an unteachable and independent spirit, going around with an attitude that he has an in-line with God. But it does mean that we can recognize that we are beginning to know God for ourselves. As a result you can be a blessing to the body of Christ. As we hear the word preached, we can acknowledge that we were also hearing the Lord all week saying the same message. The preached word should become a confirmation that what you individually are hearing from the Lord, is correct. What a secure feeling! God has one mouth. There is only one Holy Spirit.

DULL OF HEARING

When God saves us, He gives us good ears. But without exercising these spiritual ears, our hearing grows dull. The writer of Hebrews addresses this problem.

> "Of whom we have much to say, and hard to explain, since you have **become dull of hearing.**"
>
> Hebrews 5:11

The obvious implication is that these Christians had good hearing at one time. There is a marvelous innocence portrayed in a newly born-again child of God. No matter the physical age, he is like a new born infant. Although the baby doesn't have wisdom or experience, he does possess an amazing ability to hear. His own spirit is equipped with very sensitive spiritual ears.

For example, as a pastor, new Christians would come to me with the desire to be baptized in water. Upon asking them questions, I found that no one had told them or even showed them the Biblical command regarding water baptism, but each one had been individually dealt with by the Holy Spirit to be baptized in water. Each one's own spirit was sensitive to the Holy Spirit!

This type of activity was never meant to cease, but rather to be an ongoing part of the Christian life. Hearing from God should not be rare and abnormal, but commonplace. The writer goes on to say in a rebuking tone,

"For though by this time you ought to be teachers, you need someone to teach you **again** the first principles of the **oracles** of God; and you have come to need milk and not solid food. For everyone who partakes only of milk is unskilled in the word of righteousness for he is a babe. But solid food belongs to those who are of full age, that is, those who by **reason of use** have their senses exercised to discern both good and evil."
Hebrews 5:12-14

In other words they had stopped growing! Had they not become dull of hearing they would have been able to teach others by this point. But they had remained milk-drinkers, and thus continued as babes. Churches are full of babes today. They are precious people, but have not grown spiritually. But it is not their fault! It is the fault of the five-fold ministry that has not taught people that they can hear from God.

Discerning both good and evil simply represents the ability in our own spirits to recognize something that is of the Spirit or **not** of the Spirit. Many plans of man,

71

although applauded by many, cannot be considered good unless the Holy Spirit was the originator of the ideas. God's kingdom cannot be built on good ideas or enthusiasm, but must be built by men and women who have heard directly from God and are acting upon His directives.

SERMONS DON'T MAKE YOU GROW

In my first year as a pastor, the Lord spoke to my wife and me that we were to see every member of our congregation as a potential minister. Our vision was to encourage people to grow into a knowledge of God. Our job description was simple. **We were to work ourselves out of a job!** We were to teach by impartation and example by moving in the Holy Spirit.

This, of course, does not mean to teach people to defy authority and to live a spooky kind of existence with some misty-eyed religious look on their faces. Rather it means to teach people to endeavor to listen to the Lord, and to exercise their sspiritual man. The job of the five-fold ministry is to equip the saints for the work of the ministry.

> "And He Himself gave some to be apostles, some prophets, some evangelists, and some pastors and teachers, for the **equipping of the saints for the work of ministry,** for the edifying of the body of Christ."
>
> Ephesians 4:11-12

The equipment that the saints need is not books and manuals. (However, there is not necessarily anything wrong with them.) But the equipment is learning to know God, to recognize His voice, to function in the gifts of the spirit, to minister in compassion and wisdom, to understand the ways of God, to avoid pitfalls, and to be sensitive to the moving and flow of the Holy Spirit.

This is not imparting head knowledge, but rather imparting spiritual understanding. Paul made a statement to the church at Rome,

> "I long to see you, that I may **impart to you some spiritual gift**, so that you may be established."
>
> Romans 1:11

Paul knew that he would have to be there in person to impart to them a portion of the life of God that was already flowing through him. It was not a case of imparting head knowledge, but imparting the life of God.

The purpose of sermons is not to make us grow, but rather to make us clean!

> "...just as Christ also loved the church and gave Himself for it, that He might sanctify and **cleanse it with the washing of water by the word**."
>
> Ephesians 5:25-26

> "You are already **clean** because of the word which I have spoken to you."
>
> John 15:3

The anointed articulation of preaching the gospel has a way of cleansing us and destroying the bondages that cling to us. We can walk away saying, "I needed that." But growth does not come from hearing it! Growth comes from **acting** upon the word of the Lord. Whether He has said it to you through a preached word, or has spoken specifically to your spirit, you will not grow until you obey.

THE TEACHER WITHIN

The most exciting aspect of the new covenant is stated both in Jeremiah 31:34 and Hebrews 8:11.

> "None of them shall teach his neighbor and none his brother, saying, 'Know the Lord,' **For all shall know Me**, from the least of them to the greatest of them."

If it is God's desire that we come to know Him then we have to recognize the Holy Spirit as the Teacher. Twenty-four hours a day we are in a learning process. We are in the school of the Holy Spirit. He is not only available to teach us but to help us. If we go through an unpleasant experience, we should pray, "Lord, what am I to learn from this?" If we listen and learn, we won't have to learn it again.

It seems that we spend a lifetime learning that God is smarter than we are. How much trouble we save ourselves when we begin to take heed to the voice within.

This does not mean that we cannot hear from God through someone else. Nor does it mean that we disregard those whom God has put in authority over us. It means that we begin to take responsibility for our lives, by becoming responsive and responsible to God who is our Teacher within.

6

Different Ways God Speaks

*—Hearing from God should be a normal
occurrence for every Christian.*

*"...That He might make you know that man shall not live by
bread alone; but man lives by **every word that proceeds** from
the mouth of the Lord."*   Deuteronomy 8:3

We are frequently approached by people who always
ask the same question, "How do you hear from God?"
Much of that subject has been covered in this book;
however, I thought I would list several of the specific and
more common ways that God does communicate with us.

God is practical. He has a way of making things
plain to each individual. In our natural lives, we
communicate to others in a variety of ways. For example
we can speak verbally, we can wave or make a signal with
our hand, a certain look in the eye has a meaning, a
raised eyebrow, a nod, or various facial expressions. God
too, can communicate to us in a variety a ways. The good
news is, we can hear Him as we become attentive to
listen.

Many times I've heard various ones preach and
refer to the Scripture that God says in the last days He
would pour out His Spirit on all flesh. But usually, the
preacher stops there. However, it is interesting what that
Scripture from Joel, which Peter quoted from, continues
to say.

"And it shall come to pass in the last days, says God that I will

> pour out of My Spirit on all flesh; **(and) Your sons and your daughters shall prophesy,** your young men shall **see visions,** your old men shall **dream dreams,** and on My menservants and on My maidservants I will pour out My Spirit in those days; and they **shall prophesy.**"
>
> Acts 2:17-18

As God talks about His Spirit being poured out on all flesh, He equates it with hearing God! The first thing that happens when the Spirit moves is that people begin to hear God. Both male and female will prophesy, young men will see visions, and old men will dream dreams. Notice He does not say only ministers, or only prophets or apostles. But when the Spirit is poured out, it is evident that God will speak to **all** of His people. "...For all shall know Me, from the least of them to the greatest of them." Hebrews 8:11

One final note, God is spiritual and all things given by Him must be spiritually interpreted. Therefore it is of utmost importance to always pray for interpretation and spiritual understanding.

> "These things we also speak, not in words which man's wisdom teaches but which the Holy Spirit teaches, comparing spiritual things with spiritual."
>
> I Corinthians 2:13

1. THROUGH HIS WORD

Obviously the primary way God speaks to everyone is through His Word. His Word is His will. Equally as obvious, is that the best way to understand what an author is saying is to know the author personally. The same Holy Spirit who inspired and anointed the various writers, can anoint us with understanding to perceive what He is saying. Without the Holy Spirit bringing His word to life, it is more like a history book, or reading a letter from someone you have never met, written to someone else you have never met.

It is good to pray continually for the Holy Spirit to reveal and give insight into the meaning of the Scriptures, as Paul prayed for the Ephesian church.

> "That the God of our Lord Jesus Christ, the Father of glory, may give to you the spirit of wisdom and revelation in the knowledge of Him, the eyes of your understanding being enlightened; that you may know what is the hope of His calling, what are the riches of the glory of His inheritance in the saints."
>
> Ephesians 1:16-17

2. PEACE

A common way that God speaks is by giving peace or the lack of peace concerning what we are praying about.

> "And let the peace of God rule (act as an umpire) in your hearts, to which also you were called in one body; and be thankful."
>
> Colossians 3:15

In prayer, while seeking God for direction about a specific decision, He will speak by His peace. There may be a sudden deep down lack of peace or caution in your spirit. (Not in your brain, because it is impossible for the brain to figure out the mind of the Spirit). This sinking feeling or lack of peace is God saying "No" or "Something is wrong."

On one occasion, I had spoken with a man who said he could repair the church roof. He quoted me a fair price and as we stood in the parking lot of the church talking about it, I suddenly had a sickening and sinking feeling in my Spirit. But not wanting to offend him (my reasoning mind interfering), I told him to go ahead. Even as I walked away the sinking feeling remained. It turned out to be a disaster. The roof leaked worse than before. When I called him to return and repair it, he told me his pickup had broken down, which I knew was a lie and I would never see him again. Fortunately it was not a large sum of money and I knew from then on to take heed to those sinking (lack of peace) feelings.

Of course, God often will manifest His peace in such a dimension that we know we are in His will in that situation. At those moments when He speaks that way by flooding my spirit with peace, all doubt is removed. His peace is equal to His voice with the same certainty as a child receiving a hug from his mother or father.

The peace of God is to be differentiated from peace with God. Every blood-washed Christian should have peace with God.

> "Therefore, having been justified by faith, we have peace **with God** through our Lord Jesus Christ."
>
> Romans 5:1

Thank God we can enjoy His peace daily. There is no condemnation!

3. JOY

There is joy in the will of God. There is a deep down joyful satisfaction anytime you obey the Lord. Joy is part of the very nature and character of God. Therefore it stands to reason that when God is speaking to you, whatever He says to you would include joy. His will is good. "I delight to do thy will O God." Paul said,"For I delight (joyfully) in the law of God according to the inward man." Romans 7:22

There is joy in daring to believe God.

> "Now may the God of hope fill you with all **joy and peace in**

78

believing, that you may abound in hope by the power of the Holy Spirit."

Romans 15:13

When Mary entered the house of Zacharias and Elizabeth after her visitation from the angel Gabriel, the babe in Elizabeth's womb leaped for joy.

"And it happened, when Elizabeth heard the greeting of Mary, that the babe leaped in her womb; and Elizabeth was filled with the Holy Spirit."

Luke 1:41

When you hear from God, His joy in your inner man will confirm that it is His will which He is speaking about. Joy is one way He speaks and affirms what you are hearing is true.

4. HEARING WORDS IN YOUR SPIRIT

A significant way God speaks is by speaking a word or a few words to the inner man. Rarely have I ever known the Lord to speak more than a sentence in this manner. But a word or two or sentence from God can explode with meaning in your spirit. When the Spirit is moving in a meeting, often He will reveal needs to me this way. I will simply hear the words inaudibly in my spirit, such as; gall stones, left ear, hip joint, marriage problem, birthmark, cataract, etc. The voice of the Lord is simply coming in the form of word of knowledge to reveal things that God is healing.

When my wife and I put a contract on a home we were going to buy, I was concerned that it was on a street with only two other homes. Since this concerned me about buying property in an area that could possibly never develop, we prayed about it. In the few moments we prayed, my wife heard the Lord say concerning the property on that street, "Prime rib." We knew immediately He was comforting us by saying that it was prime property. Within a year, seven more houses had been built on our street.

Frequently, the Lord will speak a word or a few words that need no interpretation and give clear direction. It sure makes you appreciate the Holy Spirit.

5. SEEING BY THE SPIRIT

One of the more frequent ways that the voice of the Lord comes is by picture. Many people, when they pray, see by the spirit as they are praying. Many who prophesy, prophesy according to what they are seeing by the Holy Spirit.

In the book of Hosea, this is pointed out very clearly.

"I have spoken by the prophets, and have multiplied visions; I have given symbols (similitudes) through the witness of the prophets."

Hosea 12:10

The word, similitude, as in the King James version, comes from the Hebrew word, damah, which means mental image or mental picture. Long before television, these old time prophets literally could see something like a television screen in the realm of the Holy Spirit, as they prophesied.

When I asked the Lord why He spoke this way, He reminded me of the old adage, "A picture is worth a thousand words." When the Holy Spirit gives a picture to you concerning something you are praying about, it makes it easy to remember.

6. KNOWLEDGE IN YOUR SPIRIT

When the Holy Spirit gives you a knowledge in your spirit concerning something, that knowledge is unshakeable. This knowledge is simply the voice of the Lord, and has **nothing** to do with your mental faculties. When God lets you know something, you just know. I like to say, "You just know that you know that you know."

Women seem to be more sensitive and more open intuitively to the Lord this way. They are quicker to trust what they feel on the inside. When my wife warns me about something or someone, I have learned to trust what she says. She seems to be quicker to perceive such things. Although she has no proof, her perception in these matters has proved to have keen accuracy.

Occasionally when we have to make a decision, we will pray momentarily asking for His wisdom. Even though they are often simple everyday matters, He is faithful to speak. After all, He abides within us, He doesn't come and go. Besides it is good to activate the Holy Spirit in you and exercise in hearing Him. If you can hear Him on little and less important things, it will become easier to hear Him when you are in situations where you have to hear Him. He is our Guide, no matter what we need direction on.

A few years ago, my wife and I were in a children's clothing store buying a little sportcoat for our five-year-old boy. We were excited because the store was having a large sale. When our choice came down to one of two sportcoats (one was light blue and the other a navy blue) we prayed briefly as we stood there and both felt impressed of the Lord to get the light blue one. This seemed strange because we both liked the navy one. But we obeyed what we felt, and bought the light blue one. About a week later a package came in the mail from my wife's mother. It was a gift for our son, a navy sportcoat!

The same Holy Spirit will speak just as clearly when

you are ministering to God's people. It is important to stay in tune with Him. Exciting too!

7. YOUR FEELING NATURE

Everyone has heard sermons on don't trust your feelings. But I have found that quite commonly God speaks to our feeling nature. If a child doesn't like someone, it is impossible to talk him out of his feelings. Children trust what they feel deep inside. Often their feelings prove to be quite sensible; for example, a child may feel uncomfortable being in the presence of someone who has evil spirits.

When something doesn't feel right to you deep in your inner being, it is good to take heed to those feelings. It may well be the Holy Spirit in you trying to protect you from something. Conversely, when something does feel right, there is a sense of deep down assurance, no matter what your reasoning tries to tell you differently.

Most everyone can think of times when they just didn't "feel right" about something and it proved to be true. You can always trust the Holy Spirit.

Of course our feeling nature is different from the whims of our emotions. Emotions can change in a moments notice. But the voice of the Lord in our spirit will never lie. We must learn to discern the difference. "My sheep know My voice."

> "For the word of God is living and powerful, and sharper than any two-edged sword, **piercing even to the division of soul and spirit**, and of the joints and marrow, and is a discerner of the thoughts and intents of the heart."
>
> Hebrews 4:12

8. DREAMS

God has always used dreams to communicate to His people. He spoke to Joseph in a dream concerning using him to bring Israel into God's provision. He spoke to Jacob when he used a rock for a pillow at Bethel. He warned Joseph in a dream telling him to flee to Egypt as Herod desired to kill the Christ child. (Matthew 1:13)

Today it is common for God to speak to us in dreams. (Joel 2:28, Acts 2:17).

Dreams seem to fall into three categories. First, there are dreams of instruction or teaching. These dreams usually need interpreting and are the Holy Spirit giving wisdom and instruction concerning spiritual principles. He that keeps Israel neither slumbers or sleeps, and your spirit doesn't need sleep, so God simply gives instruction this way in the night.

The second type of dream is of the prophetic nature. This is God speaking to you something that is to come in your life. It may include direction and preparation for His purpose for you. Usually these need no interpretation, but are fairly obvious. I was clearly spoken to in a dream to resign the pastorate of the church where I had pastored for eight years. At the end of the dream the Lord spoke to me to take a giant leap of faith and leave my comfortable place. The results were glorious, as He led us into a traveling ministry.

The third type of dream is that of a warning. Several times I have been warned in a dream not to take a certain step of action, as the results would hinder what God desired to do. I was warned in a dream not to buy a piece of property for the church, which we had already made plans to buy. As I heeded the warning, God gave us free use of other property within a few months.

My wife had a very directive word from the Lord in a dream —a word of direction for someone else. In the dream the Lord spoke to her to go find a certain man.

She had heard of the man and his ministry, but had never met him. Many consider him a true prophet of God. In the dream she asked several people where he was. Someone finally said, "Go look in the prison." She found him in a cell, but the door was wide open. The Lord spoke to her to tell him, "I release you, you are free to go."

As she awakened from the dream, the anointing was so strong that she made a few phone calls, to find the man's address, and then wrote to him about the dream. Later the minister confirmed the entire situation. He was in a legalistic church, which had put him under severe bondage. He was trying to submit to it, but knew it wasn't right. The dream confirmed to him, that he was to totally break ties. He knew the dream was from God as he had never heard of my wife, and it described his situation perfectly.

Always pray for interpretation! I have known people to make foolish mistakes, assuming that God meant something that He didn't, when they didn't stop to pray for the interpretation of the dream. Some dreams seem foolish or even frightening until you realize what God is saying. Remember when interpreting dreams that God is often speaking spiritually and therefore things and people are often representative of something. For example, someone in the dream who is of spiritual authority, such as a pastor, usually represents the Lord. Animals usually represent the flesh, etc.

9. VISIONS

A vision is different from simply seeing a picture or impression in the Spirit. A vision is more of a third dimensional experience. A similitude (Hosea 12:10) could be more compared to looking at a photograph, while a vision would be like actually being there. In the book of

Acts, there are several accounts of visions. Visions too, are common as a part of the promise in Acts 2:17. I had a clear vision early one morning, upon waking up. With my eyes wide open I saw the title of a book. Instantly there was a knowledge that I was to give a copy of this book to a certain pastor. Later I heard that He was seeking God on the specific subject that the book was about. He knew it was a real answer from God to him.

Colors usually have meanings in visions and dreams. Red denotes the power of God (the blood of Jesus). Green denotes peace (He makes me to lie down in green pastures). Blue denotes the depth of the Holy Spirit (as when you look at an ocean or lake water in depth, it looks blue; and the sky appears blue in depth). White represents the purity of the Holy Spirit. Yellow denotes joy. Black usually denotes bondage or tradition. There are many other ways and symbols that God uses to speak to us. The Holy Spirit will make real to each individual how to hear what God is saying and how to interpret what He says. We all grow and develop in spiritual perception and understanding. God gives more as we are faithful to walk in what we know and to exercise our spiritual man in what He has already revealed to us.

Remember that the natural mind cannot comprehend the things of the Spirit. We are all learning to subject our minds to the mind of the Spirit.

> "Because the carnal mind is enmity (hostile) against God; for it is not subject to the law of God, nor indeed can be."
>
> Romans 8:7

The devil is defeated. We are victorious as we abide in the presence of the Lord.

> "And when he brings out his own sheep, he goes before them; and the sheep follow him, **for they know his voice.** Yet they

will by no means follow a stranger, but will flee from him, **for they do not know the voice of strangers."**

John 10:4-5

7

Feeling Good About Yourself

—You can only receive from God what you feel rightly belongs to you as a son.

"To the praise of the glory of His grace, by which He has made us **accepted** in the beloved."   Ephesians 1:6

Have you ever applied for a loan, and finally heard those glorious words, "You've been approved?" What a relief. But there is better news. God has approved you! Of course it has nothing to do with your performance, but it is by His grace.

"Not by works of righteousness which we have done, but according to His mercy He saved us..."
                                                                Titus 3:5

It is normal to desire approval from parents, from friends, employers and many other contacts in our lives. However, many struggle in religious activity and performance, subconsciously trying to win approval from God. But the good news of the gospel is, every blood-washed Christian is approved. We have been accepted. We are members of His family.

Therefore, we must encourage ourselves with this fact. We never should serve God for acceptance, but rather out of love and obedience, because we have **already** been accepted.

No religious disciplines, such as fasts, prayers, late night and weekend service, or missionary trips to dangerous places, can make you any more accepted than you already are.

Yes, we should give of ourselves, seek God, be diligent, work hard, tithe, win souls, and give witness—but not for approval, but because we are serving God out of love.

WHAT ABOUT GUILT FEELINGS?

Most people battle feelings of guilt, but those feelings can be erased the more we understand the gospel. Guilt and condemnation are the leading problems that hinder the average Christian from exercising his faith. The reason these must be dealt with is that guilt-ridden people have difficulty receiving from God, because they don't feel they deserve it.

We can receive little more from God than that which we feel is rightly ours. Even when we ask in prayer beyond what we feel we deserve, and God grants the request, we will usually reject it and declare (consciously or subconsciously) "You've got the wrong person!"

I personally battled feelings of unworthiness and inferiority for years. I thought it was normal to feel inferior and especially to feel unworthy when I prayed! Looking back, it is obvious how those feelings were satanic in origin and logically so, because if Satan can keep you feeling that God hasn't accepted you and blind to the fact that you are (presently) a joint-heir with Christ, he has succeeded in defeating you.

Common ways the enemy comes at every Christian is through the thought life, with such thoughts as, "If you were really a Christian, you'd be doing big things for God," and "How can you call yourself a Christian when you have certain thoughts?" Often we entertain these dastardly accusations of condemnation and beat ourselves down with feelings of inferiority and failure, to such an extent that we probably wouldn't hear God if He yelled at us.

But the good news of the gospel must permeate our entire being. We have been accepted, and His blood has made us righteous. We are royalty!

We can come boldly before His throne. Not with a sense of arrogance, but with faith and confidence that His blood is powerful enough to have removed every stain and guilt of sin, and present us spotless, irreproachable, justified, blameless, righteous and victorious before Him. That is the gospel. That is good news!

FEELING LIKE A SON INSTEAD OF A SERVANT

Before people can receive from God, they need to be edified and encouraged. They need hope instilled in their souls. This is why unbelief runs rampant in many churches. People have not heard the good news. All they have heard are the do's and don'ts and messages of legalism which are based on the old motivaton-by-guilt approach. This is nothing but human effort, from human perspective, trying to get divine results. But there is only one way to receive from God. You must feel worthy! You must feel like a son and not a servant.

The gospel is good news! Harsh and condemnatory preaching only digs a deeper trench of guilt and unworthiness in people. But I've learned that people already know their failures and frustrations. They hear it from the devil all week! We need to hear the gospel—the good news that we have been called into covenant with the King of kings and Lord of lords! We are worthy because we have been made His righteousness.

> "For He made Him who knew no sin to be sin for us, that we might become the righteousness of God in Him."
>
> II Corinthians 5:21

When the prodigal son came to his senses, he said within his heart,

> "How many of my father's hired servants have bread enough and to spare, and I perish with hunger! I will arise and go to my father, and will say to him, 'Father, I have sinned against heaven and before you, and I am no longer worthy to be called your son. Make me like one of your hired servants.' "
>
> Luke 15:17-19

But **before** he could get home, and was still a long way off, his father came running to him and fell on his neck and kissed him with compassion.

When our hearts turn toward God with repentance, we can't get back to the Father's house, because He is already running to meet us.

His father didn't condemn him, but rather built him up. He showed love and affection toward him. Why? Because in order for the son to be able to receive from the father as a son, he had to feel worthy. The father knew he couldn't put the best robe on one who felt as a servant. In his state of unworthiness, he would not perceive himself as a son.

The Father wants us built up and edified so we can receive the promises.

Too often we pray in a manner of a servant rather than as a son. But not even God can bestow His best on those who feel unworthy. We must hear the good news! We have already been accepted! All things have been freely given to us, because through the shed blood of Jesus Christ we are worthy to receive.

> "He who did not spare His own Son, but delivered Him up for us all, how shall He not with Him also freely give us all things?"
>
> Romans 8:32

ASSUMING RESPONSIBILITY

Many battle feelings of failure. But there is no such thing as a failure in the kingdom of God. There are two types of Christians. Those who take responsibility for their lives, and those who refuse to take responsibility for their own lives and actions.

God has no problem with mistakes. He only has a problem with those who refuse to admit their mistakes. Mistakes are inevitable for anyone who is endeavoring to follow God. However, if one is willing to take full responsibility for all mistakes, not blaming them on someone else, mistakes simply become learning experiences. Acknowledged mistakes are simply kingdom training!

Being free to fail is a luxury that God has given us, but we have not given one another. We will never grow in spiritual strength and fortitude until we give ourselves the freedom to fail.

There is no condemnation or accusation by God upon anyone who is endeavoring to walk in the Spirit.

> "Therefore there is now no condemnation—no adjudging guilty or wrong—for those who are in Christ Jesus, who live not after the dictates of the flesh, but after the dictates of the Spirit."
>
> Romans 8:1 Amplified

As we begin to receive God's love into our lives, shaking off all guilt and sense of failure, and acknowledge the Holy Spirit as our Teacher, everything is simply a learning and growing experience. The good news of the gospel is that we are free, and that includes the freedom to fail! Just accept responsibility for the failure and learn from it.

When we refuse responsibility, then we are refusing

to grow and therefore open ourselves up to condemnation again.

What happens if I miss God? Admit it! What if I thought I heard from God and I didn't? Admit it. What if not every one receives your ministry? Accept it and be glad for those who do. There are over four billion people in the world.

Many are walking around under a terrible burden of guilt, because they have refused to accept responsibility for wrong decisions they have made.

Especially in our society, it is always someone else's fault. Rarely do you hear a public official, or a business person, or those in a position of leadership in our society stand up and say, "It was my fault, and I want to take full and complete responsibility for my actions."

The prodigal son blamed no one else. He said,

"I will arise and go to my father and say to Him, 'Father, I have sinned **against heaven and before you.**'"

Luke 15:19

He didn't blame God, or those whom he had sinned with, or a family member. He simply repented, and took responsibility for his sin. King David never blamed Bathsheba, Uriah, or anyone else. He didn't even blame the circumstance which tempted him. He repented unto God.

"Against **You, You** only, have I sinned, and done this evil in **Your** sight..."

Psalm 51:4a

God is quick to forgive.

"Let the wicked forsake his way, and the unrighteous man his thoughts; Let him return to the Lord, and He will have mercy upon him; and to our God, for He will **abundantly pardon.**"

Isaiah 55:7

God holds no grudges! He will run to meet us and celebrate with us as soon as our heart turns.

KNOW GOD IS ON YOUR SIDE

I grew up always believing that I would never be able to totally please God. I felt guilty a large percent of the time. Looking back, I realize it was a harsh spirit of condemnation from the devil that I was perceiving, and was deceived into thinking it was God's feelings toward me.

My concept of God was that He followed strict rules and the ones He really loved were those who followed the rules the best. What a deceptive picture the devil (and religion) had painted in my mind!

How difficult it is to have faith in God if you believe He is impossible to please.

Therefore when we go before the Lord to pray for a need or for guidance, we must not only know that He is righteous, but that he also has declared **us** righteous through His own blood. Because of His blood we can come boldly before Him.

"Therefore, brethren, having boldness to enter the Holiest by the blood of Jesus."

Hebrews 10:19

When we go to God with a request or even a question, we must know that He will give it to us without resenting it.

If we maintain a deceptive picture that He wants to keep us in the dark concerning what we are asking wisdom for, we will probably hear nothing. But if we come unashamedly and boldly, there is no doubt that we will hear from Him. Even as we ask! He has made us worthy to receive!

> "If any of you is deficient in wisdom, let him ask of the giving God (Who gives) to everyone liberally and ungrudgingly, without reproaching or faultfinding, and it will be given him."
>
> James 1:5 Amplified

When we know that God **wants** to tell us, we can have faith that He **will** tell us. Faithlessness and wavering come from not believing that He is more than willing to grant us the request. God doesn't resent our request, rather He is going to answer liberally and generously, as we pray.

> "Only it must be in faith that he asks, with no wavering—no hesitating, no doubting. For the one who wavers (hesitates, doubts) is like the billowing surge out at sea, that is blown hither and thither and tossed by the wind."
>
> James 1:6 Amplified

A double-minded person is not convinced that God will talk to him. He is doubting the goodness and willingness of God. He doubts if he is worthy to receive an answer from God. At one point he believes that God is available to Him and means what He says. But with the next thought he doubts that God cares enough to speak personally to him. But God says, "Make up your mind!" "Become convinced that I will talk to you!" If you are not settled with that in your mind, you will be a double-minded man, and thus unstable in all you do.

Faith is not something we work up. Faith is accepting the fact that God is **willing** to do it. And that He has made **you** worthy to receive it!

We must be confident in the awesomeness of His love and in the fact that He hears us and answers us when we pray. When we pray with confidence, we know that He is attentive to us. Our confidence comes from believing the gospel. He has annihilated our sins and declared us righteous.

"Now this is the confidence that we have in Him, that if we ask anything according to His will, He hears us. And if we know that He hears us, whatever we ask, we know that we **have** the petitions that we have asked of Him."

I John 5:14-15

WHAT CHILDREN KNOW

One day my young son was so insistent upon my buying him something that I tried to reason with him that I didn't have the money. His confidence was so great that he simply said to me, "Write a check!"

Confidence comes from knowing **who** you are. A son has confidence that his father will withhold no good thing from him. Children ask with a boldness because they know they are family members, and they feel good about it. They feel like they deserve what they are asking for!

Never do you hear a child say, "Dad, how's your bank account?" He just thinks you have an endless supply. He doesn't concern himself with where and how it is going to come from, but just to get you to say you'll do it.

PRAYER IS NOT ASKING GOD TO DO WHAT HE'S ALREADY DONE

Before we ask, God has already said yes to His promises.

"For all the promises of God in Him are Yes, and in Him Amen, to the glory of God through us."

II Corinthians 1:20

Much of our prayer sounds as if we are trying to get God interested in meeting our need. But as far as God is concerned, that issue has already been settled. Provision has already been made through His blood to meet all needs. Therefore prayer is moving into the presence of

God to find that point of release. If a rich relative had deposited thousands of dollars in a bank account in your name, you wouldn't need to go through a lot of explanation convincing the teller to give it to you. It is already yours! All the teller needs is your account number and the proper identification. Prayer is releasing that provision to you. Your account number is faith and confidence that it is rightfully yours. Your proper identification is written in the Lamb's Book of Life.

ALL THINGS ARE YOURS

A major problem in Christian circles is that of holding certain leading figures in too high regard. As the world, we seem to be awed by so-called big names. Although it is good to honor those worthy of honor, I believe that the Spirit is grieved by an unhealthy allegiance and recognition of Christian personalities. This can borderline on idolatry, as we emulate excessively those whom God has used.

For one thing, God is jealous over us and desires to reveal Himself through each of us in a unique way. God uses people to provoke us unto Him, but not so we can imitate those He uses. God is too creative to have to resort to duplicates of a "popular" vessel He has used.

Secondly, eulogizing others keeps us from experiencing our own level of faith in God. Whatever belongs to others, also belongs to you as well.

> "Therefore let no one glory in men. For **all things are yours:** whether Paul or Apollos or Cephas, or the world or life or death, or things present, or things to come- -all **are yours.** And you are Christ's, and Christ is God's."
>
> I Corinthians 1:21-23

When God uses anyone in our lives, His purpose is to stir us unto Himself. As a result, our own experiences in God will increase and our faith will be stretched. If we only admire and emulate the one God used, we have missed the point.

God desires that we feel like His sons. When we feel like sons, we not only feel good about God, we feel good about ourselves. We no longer have to pray with a question mark, but can come boldly to Him. He is our Father. That is something to feel good about!

8

Are We Returning to Legalism?

—Legalism is a substitute for listening to the
Spirit.

"I do not set aside the grace of God; for if righteousness
comes through the law, then Christ died in vain." Gal. 2:21

"For I say to you, that unless your righteousness exceeds the
righteousness of the scribes and Pharisees, you will by no
means enter the kingdom of heaven." Matthew 5:20

A six year old boy stood at the altar, sobbing in
heartfelt acknowledgment of repentance and dedication
to Jesus Christ. His own father, a devout Christian, as was
the whole family, asked the boy after the meeting. "Son, I
thought you already were a Christian." The boy replied, "I
was a Christian, dad, I just wasn't saved."

This story capsulizes the classic misunderstanding
of Christianity. Christianity is an experience with a living
God, not an assent to a theology.

RETURN TO LEGALISM?

Two years ago, I listened to a prominent minister
give a prophetic warning to the church. The warning was
that the body of Christ is in danger of returning to
legalism: Multitudes would flock to the security of
religious legalism following a great shaking in the
church. True to the prophet's words, I have seen this
come about. As ministers in the public eye received

extreme media coverage about their moral failure and the handling of finances, many responded by returning to the bondage and "safety" of legalism. This would seem to almost be a reasonable response, as fear has begun to grip the church.

But we must not be deceived. There is only one way to proceed in God! We cannot move in Him by the flesh, but only by the direction of the Holy Spirit. Is this type of living risky? Yes! But there is no alternative. We cannot hide or escape under the security blanket of shallow religious legalism. We must endeavor to listen to the Spirit daily at any cost, or we will miss out on what God is doing.

Paul rebuked the Galatian church on such a closely- related matter, when many were turning back again to former customs of circumcision to attain righteousness. As today, it almost seemed easier for the people to return to the old ways, rather than moving into new frontiers of walking by the direction of the Holy Spirit.

"Stand fast therefore in the liberty by which Christ has made us free, and do not be entangled again with a yoke of bondage. Indeed I, Paul, say to you that if you become circumcised, Christ will profit you nothing."

Galatians 5:1-2

Let us take heed to this warning. Let us not return to the yoke of religious bondage. Rather, let us breathe in the fresh flow of the Holy Spirit and embrace His movement in the earth. The flesh cannot perfect us. Only the Spirit can lead us into true freedom.

"O foolish Galatians! Who has bewitched you that you should not obey the truth, before whose eyes Jesus Christ was clearly portrayed among you as crucified? This only I want to learn from you: Did you receive the Spirit by the works of the law, or by the hearing of faith? **Are you so foolish? Having begun in the Spirit, are you now being made perfect by the flesh?"**

Galatians 3:1-3

JESUS DESCRIBED RIGHTEOUSNESS AS A RELATIONSHIP

"Jesus said to him, 'You shall love the Lord your God with all your heart, with all your soul, and with all your mind. This is the first and great commandment. And the second is like it: "You shall love your neighbor as yourself." **On these two commandments hang all the Law and the Prophets.'"**

Matthew 22:37-40

In the mind of the average person righteousness is perceived as doing good and avoiding evil. In fact, in the minds of many sinners, the thought prevails when they are asked about the state of their souls, "I am basically a good person." Therefore, the bottom line is that most people view righteousness in terms of do's and don'ts. Even a non-Christian who views himself as a good person, would reason that the do's in his life outweigh the don'ts.

Christians think this way as well. We feel more righteous when we do good deeds, and we have a tendency to feel less righteous when we don't live up to these expectations.

We think that if we do enough good and avoid enough evil that we will accumulate a sufficient amount of righteousness.

Of course this line of thinking is not Biblical at all. It is a counterfeit to the real meaning of righteousness.

"Not by works of righteousness which we have done, but according to His mercy He saved us, through the washing of regeneration and renewing of the Holy Spirit, whom He poured out on us abundantly through Jesus Christ our

101

Saviour, that having been justified by His grace we should become heirs according to the hope of eternal life."

Titus 3:5-7

No longer can we define righteousness in terms of do's and don'ts. We have been justified by His grace and therefore all righteousness has been credited to our account. We don't have an inferior righteousness. We have the same righteousness as God. But it wasn't earned by our performance, it was freely given by His grace.

WE ARE GOVERNED BY A HIGHER LAW

Once we see past the the do's and don'ts and should's and shouldn'ts we realize that we are governed by a higher law, which is the life of God Himself!

"For the **law of the Spirit of life in Christ Jesus** has made me free from the law of sin and death."

Romans 8:2

No longer are we governed by "have to's," we are governed by the Spirit of God Himself. We live by that higher law that Jesus summed up all the law in,"You shall love the Lord your God with all your heart, with all your soul, and with all your mind," and "You shall love your neighbor as yourself."

Therefore, the core of the law is love. Love begins to govern us. Do's and don'ts are not the issue. The issue is whether we are loving God with all our hearts. When love becomes the issue, we desire to please Him in all our ways. No longer do we do something just because it is required, but because we want to please and glorify God.

WHAT ABOUT SIN?

Sin is no longer breaking rules. Sin is violating our relationship with God. Sin is rejecting the Spirit of God within us who desires to govern our lives. God wants the heart of man. He wants to rule from the core of our being. It is **easier** to keep requirements, because they become a substitute for living in transparent fellowship before God. Jesus rebuked the Pharisees by saying,

> "Well did Isaiah prophesy of you hypocrites, as it is written: This people honors Me with their lips, But **their heart is far from Me**. And in vain they worship Me, teaching as doctrines the commandments of men."
>
> Mark 7:6-7

It is more difficult to keep our hearts right with God and our spirits open to His voice than it is to follow rules. Therefore, living by only rules and regulations becomes a copout for walking in the Spirit.

The first thing a legalist will do if you have a problem or a weakness, is throw the law at you. But legalism is a substitute for listening to the Spirit. It becomes an easy alternative to taking the time and diligence necessary to hear what the Spirit is saying about the specific situation. Anyone can memorize rules, but only God can reveal the condition of the heart. Thank God for His mercy.

> "...For the letter kills, but the Spirit gives life."
>
> II Corinthians 3:6

THE LAW SERVES ONLY UNTIL WE BEGIN TO HEAR ON THE INSIDE

When my son comes home from school he usually forgets to put his jacket away and tosses it over a chair. When I remind him of it, he willingly (but reluctantly) puts it away. However the reason he hangs up his jacket is not because he wants to, but because he **has** to. He fears the consequences that I will deliver to him. Therefore he is putting the jacket away because of an outer law, of which he fears the consequences, which is the law of sin and death. He will be punished.

But this law does nothing for me personally! This law is only temporary! Because I have confidence that soon my boy will live by a higher law, that He desires to please me with his actions. Within his own heart will be a desire to do right. It will govern him, causing him to be responsible: not because he **has** to but because he **wants** to.

God doesn't want us to be governed by rules and requirements and regulations. He wants to govern us by His Spirit and walk in His love. As with the Pharisees, we become mindful of keeping rules and doctrines of man, but we miss the point. The bottom line is that we are to love God with all of our hearts. God wants us not to recognize the laws without, but the law of God within us.

> "For this is the covenant that I will make with the house of Israel after those days, says the Lord: **I will put My laws in their minds and write them on their hearts;**"
>
> Hebrews 8:10

Notice He doesn't say, "I will write My laws in their Bibles and in their notebooks." That is how we interpret it sometimes. But He has written His law in our minds and hearts. We have to reconcile ourselves to the fact that we must learn to listen to His voice within us.

THE LAW MAKES YOU WANT TO DO THE LEAST

When my son was small, each morning I would tell him to put his cereal bowl away when he finished breakfast. Later I would see that he had indeed put his cereal bowl in the sink, but the cereal box was still on the table and a little spilled milk as well. When I questioned him about it, he would exclaim, "You didn't tell me that, you just told me to put the cereal bowl away."

That is the epitome of the law. When we are under the law we want to do the least possible to get by. The law makes us want to do the smallest requirement possible.

104

We treat the law like a tax. We want to get by with paying the minimal amount.

LOVE MAKES YOU WANT TO DO THE MOST

However, **love makes us want to do the most.** We cannot do enough for those we love. As a child I wanted to do only what my parents required. Now as an adult, I want to do things for them, even though nothing is required. I love to go out of my way to be a blessing to them.

Jesus said to his disciples,

> "No longer do I call you servants, for a servant does not know what his master is doing; but I have called you **friends,** for all things that I heard from My Father I have made known to you."
>
> John 15:15

In the new covenant, we are not serving God out of fear of punishment. Rather we have been made joint-heirs with Him. We are laborers together **with Him.** "And they went out and preached everywhere, the Lord working with them and confirming the word through the accompanying signs." Mark 16:20.

I DIDN'T GET HERE ON MY OWN!

When the devil comes to accuse me of my weaknesses and harasses me with thoughts of unworthiness, I quickly rebuke him with these words. "It wasn't my idea to belong to God. It was His idea! He sought me out and found me! I was wallowing in my own manure pile, gratifying myself with my own lifestyle. But God reached down with His loving hand and gave me the gift of repentance and established me in his awesome grace, declaring me His own righteousness by the virtue of His own blood. He knew what He was getting when He got me (He wasn't fooled) and no matter how weak I am,

His grace is sufficient to keep me standing justified, spotless, irreproachable and blameless before Him."

We cannot even take credit for choosing God.

"You did not choose Me, but I chose you ."

John 15:16

THE LAW IS OBSOLETE

Although God has found fault with the old covenant, we have a problem of still trying to live by it.

"For if that first covenant had been faultless, then no place would have been sought for a second. Because finding fault with them, He says: 'Behold, the days are coming when I will make a new covenant with the house of Israel and with the house of Judah.' "

Hebrews 8:8-9

We still try to live by rules and regulations rather than by the new covenant principle of knowing God and allowing His Spirit to regulate us from within. But living by outer laws instead of recognizing the law of God within our hearts, is still living by the old covenant. God has declared the old covenant life-style obsolete. As we learn to live by the new covenant, we learn to **know** the Lord.

"In that He says, 'A new covenant,' He has made the first obsolete. Now what is becoming obsolete and growing old is ready to vanish away."

Hebrews 8:13

MAN WAS MADE TO LIVE BY LISTENING

I was preaching in a church in eastern Kentucky and was helping the pastor make his daily radio broadcast. After the live radio broadcast, where we talked about the goodness of God and the moving of His Spirit in the earth today, a preacher would come on after us, and try to refute everything we were saying, claiming that God no longer did the miraculous. He gave the typical ludicrous argument that signs and wonders were not for today.

The absurdity of his argument was epitomized when he made the statement, "I've been preaching for forty years, and I've never heard God one time."

This made us feel so sad, because hearing from God should be a part of every Christian's experience. No, most people do not hear Him audibly, but it should be normal to have a daily communion with God in your own spirit. Jesus said, "My sheep hear My voice."

It is not enough to have the Bible memorized, or to maintain a perfect church attendance record, or to visit people in the hospitals. While all of this is good, the Christian must have personal communion with God. He must recognize the moving of the Spirit in his life. He must recognize the voice of the Lord in his own spirit.

When Adam and Eve sinned, normal fellowship with God was broken off. No longer would they walk with God in the cool of the day. When we receive Christ, we are not receiving a fire insurance policy to protect us from hell, but rather He has reconciled us to fellowship with God the Father. Our spirits which were dead have become alive. We are reborn! We have fellowship with God. We have been reconciled to the Father. We have communion with the Holy Spirit.

> "He has delivered us from the power of darkness and translated us into the kingdom of the Son of His love."
> Colossians 1:13

GRAVECLOTHES AND RIGHTEOUSNESS

When Jesus stood at the tomb of Lazarus and called him forth from the grave, Lazarus came forth alive. However, although he was alive, he still had a need. He did not need to be resurrected again! He needed his graveclothes taken off. Jesus had given him life, but His command to the disciples was "Loose Him and let Him go." (John 11)

As Christians we are alive. We are God's righteousness. Our problem is not to be born again—again. Our problem is that we need to shed our graveclothes. That is the work of the Holy Spirit, namely His work of sanctification. We are already God's righteousness. We are saved. We are presently (not going to be) new creations. Our righteousness is a fact. It became legal and factual through the blood of Jesus. Every feeling, every action, every old habit that contradicts who God says we are, simply are graveclothes that we need to put off through the help of the Holy Spirit.

YOUR OLD MAN IS ALREADY DEAD: HE IS ONLY A MEMORY

Many people talk of dying to self or the dying of our old man (old nature). But the truth is that our old man is already dead! Our old man was crucified and buried with Jesus Christ. How then do we explain any weaknesses or unrighteous actions? They are merely the old habits—the lifestyle, that characterized our old man.

For example, when you hang around certain people, you pick up their habits and life styles. Although you are not they, you act like them, and develop habits they have and talk like them. That is what we have done. We were around our old man so long that we acquired a lot of his habits and life style. That is why Paul exhorted the Ephesians, not to kill their old man (which was already crucified) but to put off their former manner of life, that typified the character of their old nature.

"That you put off, **concerning your former conduct** the old man which grows corrupt according to the deceitful lusts, and be renewed in the spirit of your mind, and that you put on the **new man which was created according to God,** in **righteousness** and true holiness."

Ephesians 4:22-24

No longer do we have to expend all our energy trying to kill our old man, because he is already dead!

The sanctifying work of the Holy Spirit is not that God is trying to make us something that He wants us to be. Rather He is stripping off all the graveclothes that are hindering the world from seeing **who we already are!**

A story is told about an individual who picked up an old painting at a flea market for a few dollars. Upon taking it home he discovered that the paint was peeling off, and that there was another painting underneath it. He took it to a professional who spent several weeks stripping off the surface painting and discovered that the original was a priceless and famous painting that someone had painted over.

We are already new creations. We have been purchased with a great price, Jesus' own blood. We are not going to be righteous some day after great processes and trials. We are there now! We are righteous now! We are blameless now! We are forgiven now! We are justified now!

Underneath all our "weak" exterior is a priceless painting. It is a unique Designer original. It is the image of God within us.

"But we have this **treasure in earthen vessels,** that the excellency of the power may be of God and not of us."

II Corinthians 4:7

NEW LIFE OR DEAD LEAVES?

During the winter most disiduous trees loose all

their leaves. However there are a few trees, such as the pinoak trees, that keep their leaves on all winter. The dead and lifeless leaves just stubbornly hang on through those dark, dormant months.

We have two choices. We can get concerned about the ugliness and homeliness of the leaves, or we can simply choose to wait until spring when the sap rises and the new life in the tree causes new buds to spring forth. As soon as the new life begins to manifest, the old leaves simply fall off.

There are two kinds of Christians. The legalists and those who listen to the Spirit.

Legalists are blind and short-sighted. All they can see is what their senses tell them. They have no sense in their inner man of what God is saying, and so they continue to function blindly in a shallow realm trying to pull dead leaves off of Christians in a winter season.

However, the one who listens to God has a different view. Old leaves don't concern him. He sees beyond his senses. He recognizes the winter season, but he also senses that springtime is approaching. He sees no need to crawl up in the tree and pull off dead leaves, he just concentrates on new life. He knows that the life of God in the Christian will cause those old leaves, habits and lifestyles to fall off.

He is an encourager. He encourages the Christian to allow the Spirit of life to arise within Him. The legalist however just talks do's and don'ts and should's and shouldn'ts . He has no concept of life, only violations of the rulebook. Jesus described him perfectly,

"Blind guides, who strain out a gnat and swallow a camel."
Matthew 23:24

110

DEATH OR LIFE?

On one occasion while pastoring in Texas for several years, a couple in extremely poor health began to attend our church. The woman, in her late sixties, had lived with rheumatoid arthritis since she was twenty-seven years old. Her husband was also in a wheelchair having lost a leg through diabetes. They were so accustomed to sickness that it was difficult to encourage them to have faith. But the Lord spoke to us to simply love them.

Every meeting they would come in taking at least fifteen minutes to get their wheelchairs in place and get as comfortable as possible. How they loved the presence of the Lord they felt in the building! (We were so thankful that visitors often commented how they felt God's love and presence in the church). At every meeting the people poured love on this precious couple until color came into their faces and they began to radiate with the love of God.

Little by little their health improved. No, she didn't jump out of the wheelchair, but during one meeting as the saints were glorifying God in worship, something wonderful happened. Everyone was singing in the Spirit and no longer were we singing choruses, but the worship from each individual's heart flowed as the presence of the Lord told us not to stop. No song leader was allowed to quench the spirit by interrupting with a song.

At one point I looked out at the people and saw this precious woman's hands raised to God. She had not been able to lift her hands for years. But with no one demanding her to have faith, or accusing her of anything, the Lord was free to manifest His presence unto her. There were many other breakthroughs this precious couple experienced in the time they were with us before they moved to Dallas to live with their daughter. But they both left Spirit-filled, full of the love of God, and encouraged. No one did anything except to love them and to encourage them to enjoy the presence of the Lord.

A year or so before they left, a man preached in the city who had experienced a miraculous healing, and was telling about it around the country. Although he had been marvelously healed of a horrible disease, he needed more from God than what He had on the inside of him. He ministered to a group of people one night in another ·church and this lady wheeled herself up in her wheelchair to receive prayer. I believe she was asking prayer for her grandson, not about her arthritis. But this man taking one look at her and seeing her arthritis, gruffly spoke to her, "You need to read my book on forgiveness."

This innocent, God-fearing lady was so crushed. God had done so much in her, but this statement nearly broke her spirit. We had counseled with her much and never did we sense any bitterness in her heart of any kind.

However this man, having no concept of love or listening to the Spirit of God, had heard somewhere that arthritis can be caused by bitterness, and in his puny spirituality concluded that any person with any arthritis only had it because of unforgiveness and bitterness.

This minister did not have a word from God. It brought no life, no encouragement, no truth, no healing— only death. Thank God it did not destroy her, because there were wise and loving people around her to encourage her. But it could have.

My heart craves to hear God. To hear His words of encouragement and life. I'm sick of the prosecuting attorneys who call themselves preachers and preach against dead leaves because they have no concept of the life of God themselves. Born legalists, they are comfortable to hang with those who confirm their narrowmindedness and are too lazy or too stubborn to live a life open to the Holy Spirit, who gives life to the written Word of God. "For the letter kills, but the Spirit gives life." II Corinthians 3:6b

For them it is easier to live on old manna, and old covenant concepts instead of new covenant realities.

But man can only live one way. That is by communion and fellowship with God.

> "...That He might make you know that man shall not live by bread alone; but man lives by every word that proceeds from the mouth of the Lord."
>
> Deuteronomy 8:3b

If we are not communing in fellowship with God, we are only mimicking something we've heard. Then we are not a new covenant minister, only an imitator of someone else.

> "But the **righteousness of faith** speaks in this way,..... 'The word is near you, even in your mouth and in your heart'(that is, the word of faith which we preach)"
>
> Romans 10:6 and 8

LEGALISM: PRODUCES IMMATURITY AND PROMOTES IRRESPONSIBLITY

The worst thing about legalism is that it shuts out God Himself. It defies a relationship with a personal God. The gospel is not a rulebook, the gospel is a Person.

Maturity comes from listening to and fellowshipping with God. If we only see God as One who keeps records of right and wrong, then we have not seen what Jesus came for. He came to reconcile man to God Himself.

113

"That is, that God was in Christ reconciling the world to Himself, not imputing their trespasses to them, and has committed to us the word of reconciliation."

II Corinthians 5:19

LOVE SUPERSEDES THE LAW

Suppose you are driving down the interstate and you see a car accident. As you approach closer, you see a state patrolman waving you down. As you pull over and stop, he tells you that there is an emergency. A man is injured and he is not able to radio an ambulance. The patrol car is also out of commission. With your permission, he puts the injured man in the back seat of your car. The trooper gets in the front seat beside you and says, "Floor it!" He tells you to drive 80 or 90 miles an hour. Are you breaking the law? No! You are saving a life. The one with you in the car is the law, and he is telling you to forget the law and go beyond the law, that a life might be saved.

If we only minister the law to people, we will minister death. But through the Spirit, we follow a higher law that goes far beyond the law of sin and death. It is the law of the Spirit of life. This law saves lives. "For the law of the Spirit of life in Christ Jesus has made me free from the law of sin and death." Romans 8:2

When my wife and I are away from the house, we will leave notes on the refrigerator for the children. These are reminders and instructions of things they are to take care of while we are away. But when we return home, we immediately take these notes away. We are not doing away with the instruction; our presence is simply far greater than a handwritten note.

God's presence is far greater than requirements. If we love Him, we will automatically fulfill requirements, but our relationship and enjoyment of His presence are the focal point of our lives.

THE LAW IS FOR THE UNLAWFUL

The law is for those who have hardened their heart against obeying God.

"Knowing this: that the law is not made for a righteous person, but for the lawless and insubordinate, for the ungodly and for sinners, for the unholy and profane, for murderers of fathers and murderers of mothers, for manslayers, for fornicators, for sodomites, for kidnapers, for liars, for perjurers, and if there is any other thing that is contrary to sound doctrine."

I Timothy 1:9-10

Jesus did not do away with the law, He fulfilled it. (Matthew 5:17) The only way we can fulfill the law is to abide in Him.

The problem with legalism is that it destroys all expectation for the miraculous power. God desires to move in power through the church. But power will come from living in His presence and hearing what He is saying now.

"Therefore He who supplies the Spirit to you, and works miracles among you, does He do it by the works of the law, or by the **hearing of faith?**"

Galatians 3:5

The legalist's prayer: "Lord, help me be right the first time, because You know I won't change my mind."

9

Tearing Down the Gates of Hell

—Expectancy puts a demand on the presence of
God.

"The law and the prophets were until John. Since that time
the kingdom of God has been preached, and everyone is
pressing into it."   Luke 16:16

"...And on this rock I will build My church, and **the gates of
Hell shall not prevail against it.**"   Matthew 16:18

It was early in the morning and the sun was just
starting to come up. My wife and I had just begun to
pastor a church in Beaumont, Texas. Although we were
new to the city and new to pastoring, we also knew we
were in the will of God. As I came out of sleep that
morning, I clearly heard the inaudible, but distinct and
familiar voice of the Lord. He said these words to me,
**"Those looking to heaven are missing it. I'm looking for
those who have the living water flowing through them."**

Although the Lord caught me off guard, I rejoiced
in this extraordinary proclamation. I quickly got up and
wrote down those words. Those nineteen words are still
just as real today, many years later, as they were that
moment He spoke them to me. Looking back, I see that
the Lord was setting a precedence for me. He was giving
me an eternal truth. Looking to heaven is missing the
point. He doesn't redeem people for heaven, but for
Himself. What a danger the mentality of escapism is.
Heaven has never been the issue of eternal life. Jesus

117

Christ establishing His kingship and lordship over the individual heart is the issue. To have His living water flowing through us daily is the bottom line. He is searching for those who will let His Spirit flow through their lives, their conversations, their relationships, their marriages, their church services—in every part of their lives.

ZEAL FOR GOD

If God's people have one weakness more than any other, it is that of being anemic in zeal toward God. Most people are zealous and fervent in prayer when they are in some kind of trouble. When the finances are pinched, or there are family or health problems, most can pray with intensity. However, our spiritual temperature is never measured accurately in times of pressure, but is most correctly evaluated when things are going well. Those are the times when our zeal for God often evaporates.

As it was with Israel, our memory is short. How often God moved His mighty hand for Israel, then shortly after, they forgot what He had done and slid again into a lackadaisical attitude toward God.

> "In all their affliction He was afflicted, and the Angel of His presence saved them; in His love and in His pity He redeemed them; and He bore them and carried them all the days of old. **But they rebelled and grieved His Holy Spirit.**"
>
> Isaiah 63:9-10

OUTSIDERS

Frequently it was those outside of the commonwealth of Israel who expressed the most zeal toward Jesus.

Jesus Himself said, "...For the sons of this world are more shrewd in their generation than the sons of light." Luke 16:8

The centurion said, "But say the word, and my servant will be healed." Luke 7:7

The Canaanite woman with the demon-possessed daughter wouldn't leave the presence of Jesus until He granted her request, saying, "True, Lord, yet even the little dogs eat the crumbs which fall from their master's table." Matthew 15:27

What puts sluggishness into the hearts of the most blessed people on earth? It is a poor memory— the habit of quickly forgetting the power and goodness of God. We should not "cool off" spiritually in times of blessing.

> "And it shall be, when the Lord your God brings you into the land of which He swore to your fathers, to Abraham, Isaac, and Jacob, to give you large and beautiful cities which you did not build, houses full of good things, which you did not fill, hewn-out wells which you did not dig, vineyards and olive trees which you did not plant—when you have eaten and are full— **then beware, lest you forget the Lord who brought you out of the land of Egypt, from the house of bondage.**"
>
> Deuteronomy 6:10-12

HOW CAN WE MAINTAIN ZEAL TOWARD GOD?

We must desire God, more than what He can do for us. By desiring His presence and choosing to stay in His presence, we cultivate hunger for Him. Good can become the enemy of the best, so we must be on guard that the **blessing of today doesn't paralyze us for what He desires to do tomorrow.** When God fed the children of Israel the manna, they were only allowed to gather what they needed for that day. If they hoarded it, it would become moldy and full of worms. God requires a fresh dependency upon Him every day. "Give us this day, our daily bread." (Matthew 6)

Jesus said,

"And no one, having drunk old wine, immediately desires new; for he says, 'The old is better.'"

Luke 5:39

We must crave God, and despise the "little dab will do you" spiritual temperament.

MAINTAIN A SENSE OF EXPECTATION

Expectancy is to be a way of life. Nothing pleases God more than expectation. Expectancy simply means hope. Faith rests on hope. To hope means to have favorable and confident expectation. "Now faith is the substance of things hoped for, the evidence of things not seen." Hebrews 11:1

Don't be boring and religious in your relationship with God. Stay fervent toward Him. Pray with zeal. Pray with honesty. Pray with earnest expectation. Ask God to reveal Himself daily in a way that will continue to amaze you at His greatness. God always responds to the cry of a hungry soul. He will go to great lengths to satisfy him. Without faith we cannot please God, but without hope or expectancy, faith has nothing to rest on.

We have a baby girl. Her whole life involves expectation. If she sees us eating something, she simply opens her mouth, with full confidence that we will give her something. When an adult walks by she lifts up her hands in expectation that someone will pick her up. Even though she can't voice what she needs, she has expectation written all over her face.

Maintaining an awe, reverence and expectation toward God will not only please Him but will prevent your heart from becoming calloused. Many sincere and committed Christians have lost their childlike expectancy. But faith is birthed in an expectant heart. No wonder the devil would desire to paralyze the church with complacency and a heart that exerts no requisition on God.

EXPECTANCY PUTS A DEMAND ON THE PRESENCE OF GOD

When the saints come together, they must assemble with expectancy. Expectancy pulls things out of God. Expectancy puts a demand on His presence. Why should we take the time to come before God in worship, if we don't expect Him to manifest Himself?

Most have heard statements such as "Don't look for miracles." That sounds so pious, but nothing could be further from the truth. Asking God to do the miraculous is asking God to **act like God**! Telling people not to look for God to do miracles **destroys expectation!** How can God be glorified if we don't expect Him to do anything? God was glorified when Jesus healed people. He is glorified today when He moves in the church and people who came in sick leave well. The disciples dared to ask God to do signs and wonders.

> "Now Lord, look on their threats, and grant to Your servants that with all boldness they may speak Your word, by stretching out Your hand to heal, and that **signs and wonders may be done through the name of Your Holy Servant Jesus.**"
> Acts 4:29-30

Miracles are to be normal occurrences. If we live in the presence of God, God is going to act like God, and when He does, miraculous happenings will occur.

FREE TO MAKE MISTAKES

Many are bound by a fear of missing God, so they do nothing. Much teaching has implied that since we are dealing with a perfect God, we have to be perfect in everything we do in our endeavors to obey Him. We think we dare not move a muscle until we are guaranteed success. But if every move we made in response to God had a written guarantee, where would faith be? Quite frankly, if you choose to respond to God, there will be times that **you will miss Him!** But there is something worse than missing God. That is never making the effort at all!

For too long, the church has lived in this atmosphere of threatening bondage of the fear of making mistakes. But God has given us the freedom to miss Him.

What child has ever learned to walk without falling down numerous times in the process? Every child learns to walk the same way—by doing it. It would do no good to read a book to a toddler about how to walk. We can only encourage the little person to do it. The only way we learn to obey God is by doing it. If we miss Him and think we've heard His voice when we haven't, we simply repent and purpose to obey again.

A little toddler learning to walk must find his own equilibrium center. No person can tell him how to get in touch with his own sense of balance. Equally, a young Christian has to find his own center of balance in God in learning to trust and hear the voice of the Lord.

WE DON'T GROW BY WHAT WE HEAR

Contrary to popular belief, we do not grow by what we hear preached to us. We may grow in head knowledge and gain some insight, but growth comes by acting on what we've heard. In fact it is impossible not to grow if we begin to act upon the voice of the Lord to our spirit. No matter what a great orator your pastor is, or how many thousands of cassette tapes you have listened to, your spiritual growth and maturity still come primarily by having your own experiences with God.

For a minister, the issue is not how many people are listening to your sermons every week; rather the issue is how many are growing in God so much that they are hearing from God, knowing His voice and bearing fruit as a result.

The five-fold ministry has been guilty of stunting the growth of Christians for two reasons. One, because we have not given people the freedom to miss God, and secondly, we have taught people to be dependent upon us rather than trust the voice of the Lord within their own spirits.

Of course young Christians need to be properly grounded in the Word; and all Christians need to be under the anointed exposition of preaching and teaching, just as we consistently need to eat meals to stay healthy. But in order to grow spiritually, Christians must independently (not arrogantly) find their own equilibrium center in God and abandon themselves to trusting the voice of the Teacher within.

> "But the anointing which you **have received** from Him abides in you, and you do not need that anyone teach you..."
> I John 2:27

WHAT IS THE WORST THAT CAN HAPPEN?

An effective way to get up courage to obey the still small voice of the Holy Spirit, is to ask yourself, "What is the worse that can happen?" Most of the time the worse that can happen is nothing! But the best that can happen is that your action will prove to be from the Lord and there will be great results!

It is not the ultimate sin to miss the Lord. If you do, just admit it. The only thing you have to lose is damage to your ego. You are free to fail. This is not to say that anyone is to make a rash decision effecting thousands of dollars or the lives of people, just on a hunch.

However, it is important to begin to obey the Lord on small things and dare to act upon what you believe He is saying to your spirit.

For example, if you have a burden for someone, call him and tell him. Usually he will be so encouraged to know someone was praying for him, especially that God moved on you to pray. The worse that can happen, is that he says that everything was fine and he didn't need prayer. If you believe God has given you a message for someone in the church, no doubt you've heard the Lord. But rather than get in a quandary about it, go to him and deliver the message. Again the worse that can happen is the message is rejected. Even then it is not the end of the world. Conversely, it may be the very word the person needed from the Lord. Why take a chance and miss God?

Timothy was bound with fear and timidity in this area. Paul encouraged him to shake off the fear and stir up boldness in God. We too have to stir up the Holy Spirit within us.

> "Therefore I remind you to stir up the gift of God which is in you through the laying on of my hands. For God has not given us a spirit of fear, but of power and of love and of a sound mind."
>
> II Timothy 1:6-7

God gives us **power** to overcome the enemy, **love** to overcome our neighbor, and a **sound mind** to overcome our own flesh.

It is better to fall on your face while attempting to obey, than to remain in a comfortable position trying to look respectable, but in disobedience. We are more concerned about salvaging our egos than God being glorified. That is why we don't see more of the supernatural manifestations of the Holy Spirit.

God will not condemn us for our mistakes as long as we are moving toward Him with sincerity of heart. Obedience to the Spirit is the only way we will increase the kingdom of God. As we choose to obey God with sincerity of heart, He will compensate for the defects in our performance.

PRESS IN!

Often we miss the blessing God has for us because we do not press in for the manifestation that we need. God is a rewarder of those who diligently (not casually) seek Him (not seek faith).

Children know how to press in for what they want. They just keep asking! Observing my own children, I have concluded that children have only one motive from the time they wake up in the morning until they go to bed at night. That one motive is to get the parent to say, "Yes." In fact children don't even care if they make you mad in the process. They just want permission! They ask with desire and intensity, often which results in getting their request granted. A child knows he cannot get a job, and doesn't have the ability to get what he desires. His only option is that of his parent's granting the request. Therefore, that is where he puts all his energy, to get the parent to make a promise. Children know that you, the parent, are equal to your word. When a child has his parent's word on something, to him, that is equal to the manifestation. In his eyes, the parent cannot break his word.

So too, with God. He is equal to His word.

Therefore if He tells you something, whether through a prophet, by speaking to your spirit, or by speaking a specific scripture to you, it will come to pass.

That is why we must approach God with intensity. As a child we must come with that tenacious and resolute desire to hear a fresh word from Him.

DON'T LOSE HEART

Many don't press in to God with their petition because they lose heart. Jesus addressed this problem.

> "Also Jesus told them a parable, to the effect that they ought always to pray and not to turn coward— faint, lose heart and give up."
>
> Luke 18:1 Amplified

There is a tendency when you first begin to pray to feel as if God doesn't want to answer your prayer. You may even feel as if He doesn't care. But Jesus addressed this problem by comparing Himself to an unrighteous judge. This judge had no consideration for man, neither did he fear God. Yet a little persistent widow kept coming to him saying "Avenge me of my adversary." Although he did nothing for her at first, he later said to himself that he would grant her petition, because he feared she would wear him out!

> "And for a time he would not; but later he said to himself, 'Though I have neither reverence or fear for God nor respect or consideration for man, yet because this widow continues to bother me, I will defend and protect and avenge her; lest she give me intolerable annoyance and wear me out by her continual coming or at the last she come and rail on me, or assault me, or strangle me."
>
> Luke 18:4-5 Amplified

The judge would only respond for one reason. Like God, he was no respecter of persons. He would give her everything she wanted because of her continual coming and persistence. Then Jesus challenges us to be persistent in our faith and prayers. They will bring speedy results.

> "And shall God not avenge His own elect who cry out day and night to Him, though He bears long with them? I tell you that He will avenge them speedily. Nevertheless, when the Son of Man comes, will He really find faith on the earth?"
>
> (vs. 7-8)

Can you see this little ninety pound widow? Each morning she is waiting for him at the courthouse steps, saying, "Sir, I need legal protection, can you help me?" Each day he walks right past her, hardened to her needs. But her response is, "I'll see you tonight." Then as he is on his way home from a busy day on the bench, she is there again, waiting for him, "Sir, can you help me please? I need legal protection." Finally at home one evening he is relaxing and begins to think, "She is going to wear me out. Although I don't care about her or anyone, and I do not fear God, tomorrow I'm going to grant her request, because she's not going away until I give her what she wants. She will wear me out in the process."

The Lord says we have to come to Him with that same persistence. Don't let up. Pray as if to wear Him out. Isaiah prophesied,

> "I have set watchmen on your walls, O Jerusalem, Who shall never hold their peace day or night. You who make mention of the Lord, **do not keep silent, and give Him no rest** till He establishes and till He makes Jerusalem a praise in the earth."
> Isaiah 62:6-7

Pray as if to say, "Lord you are not going to bed tonight until I have a promise from You that you are going to take care of my petition."

When four men brought a paralytic to Jesus, they found that the house was full.

> "And when they could not come near Him because of the crowd, they uncovered the roof where He was., And when they had broken through, they let down the bed on which the paralytic was lying."
>
> Mark 2:4

How easily they could have become discouraged and simply chalked it up as "It must not be God's will. Let's go get a cup of coffee." But instead they persevered and broke through the roof. That is what we must do when we pray. Break through! Of course you'll feel hindered and resisted, but God will help you to break through. Jesus didn't rebuke them for tearing a hole in the roof. He saw their faith! Then He forgave the man of his sins and healed him. God will help you to break through. Press in!

BE VIOLENT!

As a young pastor, I had led a woman to the Lord. She was about sixty-five years old and had no previous background of church or any type of spirituality. A few weeks after she had accepted Christ and was filled with the Holy Spirit, she came to me and said, "Pastor, the Lord gave me a message for you." I said, "What is the message?" She said, "The Lord said to tell you to tell My people that I want them to become violent." I knew immediately what the message from the Lord meant, because I was familiar with the Scriptures about violence, such as,

> "And from the days of John the Baptist until now the kingdom of heaven suffers violence, and the violent take it by force."
>
> Matthew 11:12

I knew that this lady had no knowledge of this

Scripture, and she was clearly hearing directly from the Lord. I was to begin to teach the people to press into the promises of God. As I did so, we began to hear of awesome answers to prayer as people became aggressive in their prayer lives.

Jesus said, "The thief does not come except to steal, and to kill, and to destroy..." John 10:10a Therefore we must be violent in our resisting of his trespassing in our lives. We cannot sit passively as he tries to steal our joy, or to rob from us in anyway. Don't ask him to leave, command him to go!

Before I got up to speak at a Full Gospel Businessmen's regional meeting in Illinois, a man who was introducing me gave a short testimony. He shared a recent experience where he was ready to leave on vacation and they called him from work that a major piece of highly technical equipment had broken down. As he was driving to the plant, he prayed with desperation that God would help him quickly pinpoint the problem as he had committed himself to leaving on vacation by 4:30 that afternoon. As he prayed in desperation, the Lord showed him a picture by the Spirit as he drove toward the plant, that the problem was in component number three.

When he entered the plant he told the other engineers where the problem was. They disagreed with him, saying it was not logical, but agreed to check it anyway, because they had been unsuccessful in finding the problem. As they checked the number three component they were surprised to find out that it was indeed the problem, and the problem was quickly corrected. Of course the man rejoiced as he was able to make his commitment without having to change plans.

The Lord let me see that the reason this man so easily received the answer on the problem was that he prayed violently and knew he didn't have time to lose. As he prayed knowing that the answer was a must, he was squeezed into raising his own level of expectancy, and as a result, heard from God.

However, the Lord challenged me that we could always hear that quickly if we would **become** more violent in our prayers. Don't just pray. Pray violently. Pray with expectation. Press into God to meet your need. He will move quickly in your behalf.

It is easy to become too casual in our prayers. That is why so much Scripture speaks about fervent praying. All the things of the kingdom of God are freely given to us, but we must press into the kingdom with violence and boldness, knowing that what we are asking for is rightly ours. Not that we have earned it, but that we have been given it through the Person of Jesus Christ.

> "Therefore, brethren, having boldness to enter the Holiest by the blood of Jesus."
>
> Hebrews 10:19

EMBRACE WHAT GOD IS SAYING!

How many times have I heard my own children say "But you said!" When it comes to any promise, whether insincere or not, children take you at your word. Have you ever tried to back out on a promise you made? That child will quickly remind you what you said to him that you would do, and he intends to hold you to it.

Children embrace the promise you give them, without any intention of letting it go.

JUMPER CABLES

What a bondage it would be if the battery on your car wouldn't stay charged. Can you imagine going to the grocery store, and upon coming out you had to look for someone who had a set of jumper cables? After you found someone to help boost your battery by attaching the cables from his car to yours, you drive off. But at your next stop, you are again looking for a person to help you get your car started, because the battery is dead again.

Jumper cables can be likened to prayer. It is Biblical to have hands laid on you for healing and various needs. But it is normal to keep yourself encouraged. God has made a way for us to remain in a charged state. This is done through the exercising of the prayer language He gives to the believer.

A car battery is like the human spirit, it needs to stay charged. Praying in the Holy Spirit is the generator that keeps the battery (human spirit) charged.

> "But you, beloved, building yourselves up on your most holy faith, praying in the Holy Spirit."
>
> Jude 20

When we are built up in God, our spiritual man is strong and muscular. Edified people tear down the gates of hell.

TEARING DOWN THE GATES OF HELL

Jesus responded with great satisfaction when Peter answered Him with authoritative revelation, as He asked the disciples, "But who do you say that I am?" Matthew 16:15 Peter responded, saying, "You are the Christ, the Son of the living God." (vs. 16)

It was not just the answer Jesus was looking for, but the way Peter received the answer. Peter recognized that Jesus was the Christ (not because he stayed up all night studying) but because he heard the voice of the Father.

What a milestone it was from Jesus' perspective! His disciple, Peter, had the same experience of hearing the Father that Jesus lived by. This life of listening to the Father would be the power-source of the church. As men tuned into what the Father was saying, the gates of hell would not be able to withstand the power of it.

> "Jesus answered and said to him, 'Blessed are you, Simon Bar-Jonah, for flesh and blood has not revealed this to you, but My Father who is in heaven. And I also say to you that you are Peter, and **on this rock I will build My church, and the gates of Hades shall not prevail against it.'** "
>
> (vs. 17-18)

The church's strength and priority must be that we are hearing from the Father. If we do, Satan doesn't have a chance.

If we do not hear from the Father, we are no threat to Satan's kingdom, but are merely depending upon human effort, vainly striving for divine results.

10

Joy—The Key to Receiving

—Joy is the fertile ground on which the seed of God can take root in your life.

"Sing, O barren, You who have not borne! Break forth into singing, and cry aloud, you who have not travailed with child! For more are the children of the desolate than the children of the married woman," says the Lord." Isaiah 54:1

Sometime back I went through a period of discouragement. Even though I knew better, I continued to entertain negative thoughts. During this time I could not see anything in a positive light. The littlest problem seemed to be magnified to me as an overwhelming obstacle. In my state of depression, everything seemed adverse and even hopeless.

One day during this time my wife came to me and told me the Lord had spoken to her as she came out of sleep that morning. (I had not told her about the inward battle I was having). She told me what the Lord said to her. "Depressed people see and hear in distortion."

Suddenly I saw the light. Because of the spirit of depression that I had entertained, it was impossible for me to see anything without seeing it in distortion. Depression is similar to wearing thick bifocals when you have 20/20 vision. Everything looks distorted. Of course I had to repent for entertaining the depressing thoughts, and when I did, the joy of the Lord returned.

More than ever, I understood how Christians must maintain joy in their Christian lives. We have authority over all the enemies of joy, such as depression and discouragement. The devil knows that depression will keep us from seeing and hearing things in God's perspective. Joy is what keeps our heart open to hear the voice of the Lord.

JOY IS NORMAL

Joy is normal for the Christian. God never intended for us to serve Him without joy. Joy is that intoxicated state that should be normal Christian living, and should never be absent from the church or the saints.

Just as the most expensive car still needs fuel to run, the Christian must have joy to have continual victory.

Joy is the new wine, the precious Holy Spirit. Even Paul described the kingdom of God as "righteousness, peace and joy." (Romans 14:17)

When the 120 in the upper room on the day of Pentecost were accused of being drunk with new wine, the accusers were not totally wrong. They saw the intoxication of the Holy Spirit or they would not have perceived them as drunk. But they had the wrong brand! It was the Holy Spirit who was filling them with joy.

DON'T MERELY SERVE GOD

It is not enough to merely serve God. We are to **enjoy** serving Him. No marriage could be called even mildly good unless the husband and wife were enjoying the marriage. Without enjoying it, it is no more than a tolerant union of two people, a test of endurance.

No wife would be flattered by her husband telling her that he has endured the marriage for all these years.

Yet much has been implied that we are to endure

God. But we **are** not to endure God, we are to enjoy Him. Enjoying the presence of the Lord is not an option!

> "Because you did not serve the Lord your God **with joy and gladness of heart,** for the abundance of all things, therefore you shall serve your enemies, whom the Lord will send against you, in hunger, in thirst, in nakedness, and in need of all things; and He will put a yoke of iron on your neck until He has destroyed you."
>
> **Deuteronomy 28:47-48**

WHO ARE YOUR ENEMIES?

Our enemies are not Soviet dictators. Our real enemies are fear, discouragement, depression, unbelief, and confusion. Why are these such powerful enemies? Because they rob our joy. When there is no joy, there is no strength and hope. Then it is difficult, if not impossible, to hear from God.

We must live in the presence of the Lord. If we stay in His presence, no enemy can remain.

> **"You will show me the path of life; In Your presence is fullness of joy; At Your right hand are pleasures forevermore."**
>
> **Psalm 16:11**

JOY IS PART OF THE ARMOR

A little child needs help getting dressed. He is helpless in getting his little shirt on, his little socks, and his little shoes. But every parent knows that this will change. This is only temporary. The time will come quickly when that child can dress himself.

We must learn to dress ourselves. At a certain point in our growth, God won't "dress us" any longer. He simply says, "Dress yourself!" We have to take the initiative and put on the garment of praise, the helmet of salvation, the breastplate of righteousness. Every morning we can make the decision to rejoice in the Lord, to put on the mind of Christ, and to declare that we have been made the righteousness of God.

We have been given joy to replace sadness and praise to replace heaviness, but we have to take the initiative to put them on.

"To console those who mourn in Zion, to give them beauty for ashes, the **oil of joy** for mourning, the garment of praise for the spirit of heaviness; that they may be called trees of righteousness, the planting of the Lord that He may be glorified."

Isaiah 61:3

"Awake, awake! Put on your strength, O Zion; Put on your beautiful garments..."

Isaiah 52:1

JOY IS SLIPPERY

The devil will always try to unload his goods on you. "You've had four good days, its about time you are depressed again." Or, "Did you see what they did to you?" Or, "Do you know what they are saying about you?"

But thank God for the oil of joy. The oil makes you slippery so nothing can stick to you. It just slides off. All the accusations and speculations of the enemy are of no effect because you are slippery with joy. Only the lack of rejoicing will cause the oil to dry up.

When the devil tries to hand you these thoughts, don't sign for them. Tell him he's got the wrong address.

DON'T TAKE YOURSELF SO SERIOUSLY

Laugh at yourself. Too many of us take ourselves far too seriously.

It is interesting that medical science is actually sending some terminally ill patients to laughter clinics.

They encourage people to laugh as they have learned that laughter releases chemicals in the blood stream that promote healing. They have discovered what God has said all along. Laughter is a medicine.

"A merry heart does good, like a medicine. But a broken spirit dries the bones."

Proverbs 17:22

"The light of the eyes rejoices the heart, and a good report makes the bones healthy."

Proverbs 15:30

"All the days of the afflicted are evil, but he who is of a merry heart has a continual feast."

Proverbs 15:15

When are we going to learn that stress and anxiety are abnormal? Joy and rejoicing are **normal.** Joy is to be the normal state of man. Worship is man's normal habitat. Living in the presence of the Lord is to be our normal state. God made man to be a vessel of joy, full of abundant life.

There is a great freedom in laughing at yourself. When you don't take yourself so seriously, it is easier to take God seriously. He is not intimidated by our weaknesses. He only commands us to rejoice in Him and acknowledge Him.

"Let the weak say, 'I am strong.'"

Joel 3:10

It's exciting to serve God! It's exciting to walk in the Spirit. And besides that, it's normal!

The flow of the Holy Spirit in our lives is meant to be perpetual.

David said,

"I will bless the Lord at all times; His praise shall continually be in my mouth."

Psalm 34:1

The baptism in the Holy Spirit was never meant to be the end, but the beginning. The Bridegroom has only carried you across the threshold. What God has begun will be perpetual and it will become more and more of a glorious, ongoing experience with God. Don't let the devil steal your joy. Stay in the flow of God. Stay in His presence. Just because church is dismissed, does not mean God is through. His perpetual flow is still in your inner man.

RESISTANCE BRINGS JOY

Have you ever been driving down an unfamiliar highway, feeling uncomfortable because you are not sure if you are on the right road? Then after a few miles you see a highway sign, that informs you that you are indeed on the right highway. As soon as you see that sign, you are comforted because you know you are not lost.

It is like this concerning the enemy. You begin to obey God, and are not sure you are hearing Him correctly. Then contrary things happen and it is obvious that the devil is resisting you. Rather than be upset, you feel a surge of joy, because the only reason the enemy would be resisting you is because you're on the right track. His resistance is a good sign (a road sign)!

Frequently when my wife and I are ready to go on a speaking engagement, we will feel incredible resistance from the enemy. It used to discourage us. But now we've gotten smart. We rejoice and comfort each other that the trip is going to be extra fruitful, or the devil wouldn't be going to so much trouble to resist us.

"And the word of the Lord was being spread throughout all the region. But the Jews stirred up the devout and prominent women and the chief men of the city, raised up persecution against Paul and Barnabas, and expelled them from their region. But they shook off the dust from their feet against them, and came to Iconium. **And the disciples were filled with joy and with the Holy Spirit."**

Acts 13:49-52

WHAT ROBS JOY?

Satan is the joy-robber. But how does he get his foot in the door? One way is through self-centeredness! Self- centered people are always succeptible to depression. Ten minutes of thinking of yourself, will depress anybody. The majority of mental problems can be traced back to self- centeredness. We once heard a prominent evangelist say, "Self-pity is Satan's baby sitter without charge."

Every human being is self centered, but the Holy Spirit helps us grow out of that state. One person explained it this way, that if you want to find out if you're self- centered or not, see who you look for first on a group photo!

ENCOURAGE ONE ANOTHER TO MAINTAIN JOY

We must learn to encourage one another to rejoice. How can we hear from God when we are discouraged or depressed? What good are we to anyone else if we are not encouraged ourselves?

Jesus told his disciples,

"These things I have spoken to you, that **My joy may remain in you,** and that **your joy may be full."**

John 15:11

This clearly indicates that it is possible for joy to leave. But we can encourage one another to rejoice and stay in the presence of the Lord.

Even in trials, the joy of the Lord does not depart from us. If a doctor were ready to perform surgery on you, not having administered a sedative, upon seeing him lift the scaple, you might say, "Aren't you forgetting something? What about the sedative?" If his reply was that he didn't use sedatives, you might jump off the table and run. The joy of the Lord is a pain-killer. It is the sedative that keeps us conscious of Him.

JOY MAKES THE HEART RECEPTIVE TO HEAR FROM GOD

Hearing from God is a wonderful experience. Whether He speaks to us through His Word, or directly to our spirit, or through a vision or a dream, or through another person, it is exciting to hear His voice.

A rejoicing heart is a fertile heart. When God gives the seed of His word to us concerning a specific promise, we must hear it with joy. When the angel Gabriel gave the divine announcement of good news to the virgin Mary, his first word to her was "Rejoice."

> **"Rejoice,** highly favored one, the Lord is with you; blessed are you among women!"
>
> Luke 1:28

The only thing she was commanded to do as she stood at the threshold of being such a mighty instrument in the hands of God, was rejoice. If she would rejoice, God would do the rest. Before the angel departed from her, her joyful and receptive heart declared,

> "Behold the maidservant of the Lord! Let it be to me according to your word."
>
> Luke 1:38

If we want to be an instrument that God uses to bring forth His purpose and plan, we must maintain a joyful and expectant heart.

Satan's Coloring Books

—The devil is not threatened by religious activity as long as it is not Spirit-directed activity.

"Martha, Martha, you are worried and troubled (distracted) about many things. **But one thing is needed,** and Mary has chosen that good part, which will not be taken away from her."   Luke 10:41-42

Several years ago, one of the nation's most prominent fast food restaurants was under harsh attack and being boycotted by Christians everywhere. This multi-million dollar food chain was allegedly tithing a percentage of its profit to the church of Satan in California. Months later, the company issued a statement that this was indeed a rumor and had absolutely no truth to it. The rumor was traced back to a housewife who had misunderstood a statement she heard during a radio show.

This fact came to the surface finally, but not before thousands of Christians had expended countless hours of precious energy fighting nothing; energy that could have been channeled into prayer and efforts to increase the kingdom of God.

Within a year or so of this outburst came another rallying of distracted Christians. This time it was against a prominent soap products company whose toothpaste tube had an unusual design on it, interpreted by some ardent Christian trouble-shooters to be a Satanic symbol.

After a great deal of hullabaloo this too proved to be false, but was simply a design selected by the company which, although ugly, had nothing to do with Satanism. However, again, much potentially profitable use of time, energy, and money, was squandered away on another mirage used by Satan to distract people from fruitful activity in God's kingdom.

CHICKEN LITTLES

Oftentimes, we in the body of Christ resemble the nursery- book character, Chicken Little. He was the character who, when a walnut fell out of a tree on his head, immediately took off running in a Paul Revere style proclaiming to all his presumption that the sky was falling. Many joined his frenzy and ran with him.

Today, many have the Chicken Little mentality. The devil throws out a rumor with a little sensation to it (with one main purpose)—to distract us from productive spiritual activity. Often we run, joining in the frenzy, without checking the facts. Whether it comes in the form of a rumor about the pastor, or about a movie or about a company using a weird logo, we're off and running. We bring more attention to what we are fighting (or think we are fighting) than to the Lord Jesus Christ.

SATAN'S COLORING BOOKS

Distractions are Satan's number one strategy against the Christian. This stands to reason. Since the devil cannot keep you and me from being saved or filled with the Holy Spirit, his ploy is to simply divert us into useless activity, so our energy will not be spent on the increase of the kingdom of God.

The Lord let me see clearly that the enemy's tactic is similar to that of an unruly kindergartner in a classroom. The teacher, recognizing that this child will disturb the rest of the class, needs a way to divert the child temporarily, and she does this by handing him a coloring book. Although the child is satisfied that he is busy and actually feels productive, he is learning nothing and all his energy is expended for a useless purpose. It is a perfect panacea for the teacher who has quickly and successfully gotten the little fellow out of her way so she can go on with her class.

When we begin to tune into God, we get in the devil's way. Therefore, we must be on guard against him handing us a "coloring book." The devil is not threatened by activity as long as it is not Holy Spirit directed and energized activity.

Therefore we must be on guard against the need to feel useful. If we want to do something for God, and most of us do, we must separate it from the need to feel needed and the need to feel productive. If we desire activity toward God, for activities sake (and not because we are hearing God) the devil will quickly accommodate that desire by handing us a "coloring book." While we may feel productive for awhile, in reality, the devil just got us out of his way.

NOT EVERY NEED HAS YOUR NAME ON IT

Every Christian must be careful to be God-conscious before he is need-conscious. In every church there are those who are more than willing to make themselves available to any need mentioned. And while I commend them for their willingness to be the answer to a need, I would caution them to seek the Lord that He would help them to hear His voice. Activity-centered Christianity will dwarf the Christian's spiritual growth. Misguided busyness causes spiritual barrenness.

THE NEED TO FEEL USEFUL

Many Christians are bound to a performance mentality. Although there is certainly nothing wrong with a fervent desire to please God, there is a danger of trying to supplement the work of the cross and of God's righteousness, by some deeds of our own. There is something about human nature that has a need to feel that we have contributed something to it.

Simply put, we haven't always heard clearly the gospel message. We have been made righteous through no effort of our own, except by believing in Jesus Christ. God is pleased with the Christian (regarding righteousness), only because He sees us "in" the Son. We are either "in" Christ or without Him. If we are "in" Him, we have His righteousness. However, much religious performance or activity is consciously or subconsciously trying to feel worthy of such righteousness.

Satan is quick to discern our zeal for God, and quickly accommodates our sincere, but ignorant and misdirected desire by handing us a "coloring book" of a special activity which makes us feel spiritual, but does nothing to produce fruit for the kingdom of God. In addition, such activity usurps our energy from something divinely ordained that God had intended for us.

DISTRACTIONS COME IN NECESSARY LOOKING PACKAGES

We were seeking God in preparation to minister in a New York church when the Lord spoke these words to my wife, "Distractions come in necessary looking packages." What a true statement this is. The enemy always wraps a distraction in a disguise that would make it appear to be necessary.

Distractions come in many forms, but perhaps the greatest one is ego. In our human nature (which is destined to be crucified) we suffer from an ego that is starving for credit and recognition. Only a sold-out heart will be heedful to the danger of embracing ego-rendering and ego-exalting activity. We have better things to do then working on "coloring books."

12

The Good News Covenant

—The new covenant cannot fail, because God has
made it dependent upon Himself, not upon us.

"...Behold, the days are coming, says the Lord, when I will
make a **new covenant** with the house of Israel and with the
house of Judah."   Hebrews 8:8

"Get help!" That's the first message I hear every
morning- -from the mirror. Like most of the human race,
when the alarm clock goes off, I stagger into the
bathroom and look in the mirror. The mirror is always
faithful to give me that same message. "You need help."
The message from the mirror is clear. Depending upon
who we are, it will tell us to shave or to put on makeup
and to comb our hair.

The mirror is invaluable in telling us what we need.
However, all the mirror can do for us is to tell us that we
have fallen short of perfection.

The mirror serves as the law. When we look into
the law, the law examines us and says, "You come up
short." Or, "You've failed." But once the law gives you
that abrupt message, it can do no more for you. It has one
purpose, to reveal sin, and to show you your helplessness.

"What shall we say then? Is the law sin? Certainly not! On the
contrary, I would not have known sin except through the law.
For I would not have known covetousness unless the law had
said, 'You shall not covet.' "
                                                    Romans 7:7

Upon looking in the mirror, we cannot take it off

147

the wall and shave with it, or use it to apply makeup or to comb our hair. It can only frustrate us and provoke us to get the help we need. The law can only tell us what we need. It cannot clean us up, and it cannot make us stand righteous before God. If we are guilty in the smallest aspect of it, we are guilty of the whole law. (James 2:10)

The law is only a standard by which we are measured, but it is a standard by which we all have come short. "For all have sinned and fall short of the glory of God." Romans 3:23

Although the law was never able to justify us before God, it forces us to look to the One who could!

> "For what the law could not do in that it was weak through the flesh, God did by sending His own Son in the likeness of sinful flesh, on account of sin: He condemned sin in the flesh, that the **righteous requirement of the law might be fulfilled in us** who do not walk according to the flesh but according to the Spirit."
>
> Romans 8:3-4

GOOD NEWS!

The gospel is good news. The word, gospel, means good news. Jesus said, "The time is fulfilled, and the kingdom of God is at hand. Repent, and believe in the gospel (good news)." Mark 1:15

Anytime the gospel is preached or proclaimed, it should be good news, because it **is** good news. God has chosen to annihilate our sins through the blood of His Son. All we must do, is repent and accept that they are already atoned for!

There are two covenants in Scripture, the old and the new. The old covenant was a conditional covenant. It was conditional upon our performance in obeying God's laws and following His commandments. God would allow certain blessings if people were faithful to keep their part of the covenant.

The new covenant has nothing to do with our performance and adherence to rules, rather it is based on a belief and acceptance of a performance that has already been performed and a requirement that has already been satisfied, namely the death of Jesus Christ on the cross.

The old covenant had one purpose for you and me. That purpose was to show us that we need a new covenant! The old covenant shows us that we cannot make it by our performance. That's good news!

In fact the law was added to the old covenant to further aggravate our performance, in order to bring us to the realization more quickly that we cannot do it by our own efforts, no matter how sincere they are.

No amount of prayers, fastings or scores of other spiritual disciplines could persuade God to accept us one iota more than He already has! We stand righteous before Him by simple belief and faith in the shed blood of Jesus and the fact that God raised Him from the dead.

THE GOOD NEWS COVENANT

The problem with good news is that we have trouble believing it. The good news of the gospel is such good news that it seems too good to be true. God has given us total amnesty where our sins were concerned. He has given Himself divine amnesia! We are not ex-sinners, ex-addicts, ex- pornographers, ex-adulterers, ex-alcoholics or sinners saved by grace. We are His own righteousness! No wonder Paul wrote,

> "For I am not ashamed of the gospel of Christ, for it is the power of God to salvation for everyone who believes, for the Jew first and also for the Greek. For in it the **righteousness of God is revealed** from faith to faith..."
>
> Romans 1:16-17

However, we are quicker to believe bad news than good. If the devil tells us that we are a failure, we accept that news easily. But if God tells us that we are more than conquerors, we ask Him to confirm it a hundred times. We struggle with believing such good tidings, and continue to live with low expectations of His plan and purpose for us.

We have been taught to be "on guard" against good news. If we were told that our car had been stolen, we might exclaim "I knew it." But if were told that we've been promoted, received a raise, been healed, made free from oppression or been made the righteousness of God, we might say, "I can't believe it."

The good news is that no longer does one have to perform certain actions for acceptance, but we are already accepted and righteous through the blood of Jesus. The good news covenant is not based on do's and dont's and should's and shouldn'ts, rather it is a relationship with God where we live by listening to the voice of the Holy Spirit.

God is the initiator. He initiated the solution to the sin problem before the world began. Jesus was the Lamb slain before the foundation of the world. (Revelation 13:8)

HEAVEN IS NOT THE ISSUE

The purpose of the new covenant is not to get us into heaven, but **into God!** Satan has distracted the body of Christ into an escapism mentality that has us looking to heaven instead of to God. We have not been saved from sin so we can go to heaven, or so we can avoid hell. Although both heaven and hell are realities, the blood covenant is to bring us into fellowship with God.

His covenant with us is far more than a fire

insurance policy to protect us from hell and a guarantee that we will go to heaven. God has not reconciled us **from sin** but **to Himself!**

We have been reconciled to God! **He** is our salvation and our inheritance. Christians are not an assemblage of people who believe certain facts and doctrines that others do not. Christians are a people who have been called into covenant with God. We were once not a people, but now we are the people of God.

"Who once were not a people but are now the people of God, who had not obtained mercy but now have obtained mercy."
I Peter 2:10

When heaven becomes the issue, salvation is reduced to being a place rather than a Person. How ridiculous it would sound for a young woman preparing for marriage to be consumed about thoughts of the house her new husband would provide for her to live in! Their reason for marriage is not a place to live, but the love they have for one another and that they will be enjoying life and intimacy together.

Heaven is only a by-product of our relationship and intimacy with Jesus Christ. The issue is that we have been reconciled to Him! If we have been reconciled to Him and accepted by Him by His own blood, and are choosing to follow Him by walking in the Spirit, we couldn't miss heaven if we wanted to. That's good news!

THE PROBLEM WITH PERFORMANCE

The Lord spoke to me one day that the old covenant mentality consists of striving, enduring, and performing. While the new covenant mentality consists of resting, rejoicing and listening.

The old covenant is a performance or conditional covenant. Many in the body of Christ are still tied to old

151

covenant perception and thinking, because they believe that everything God does or doesn't do is based on their performance. But the good news is that God has declared the old covenant obsolete. "In that He says, 'A new covenant,' He has made the first **obsolete**. Hebrews 8:13 We don't please God by performance, we please Him by walking in Jesus Christ and in the power of His Spirit. That is far better than performance. It is obedience. "Obedience is better than sacrifice." (I Samuel 15:22)

YOU'RE ALREADY THERE!

Much prayer sounds as if we are still trying to get God to accept us. But the good news is, He already has! But He hasn't accepted us on the basis of anything we have done, rather upon what **He** has done.

The devil tries to get us into the future. Someday you'll be righteous. Someday you'll be worthy. Someday God will heal you. Someday you'll be victorious. But that is a lie. Because of the new covenant which was brought into effect through the shed blood of Jesus, we are already new creations, righteous, victorious, worthy and all that God has is ours. It is reality. We are not going to be, we already are!

> "Therefore if anyone is in Christ, he **is a new creation**: old things have passed away; behold, **all things** have become new."
>
> II Corinthians 5:17

WHY DID GOD DO IT?

The reason the new covenant works is that He made it dependent upon Himself, not upon you and me. It is failure-proof. God pledged to Himself to have a people who would be free from sin and would know Him.

> "For this is the covenant that I will make with the house of Israel after those days says the Lord: I will put My laws in

their mind and write them on their hearts; and I will be their God and they shall be My people. None of them shall teach his neighbor, and none his brother, saying, 'Know the Lord,' **for all shall know Me, from the least of them to the greatest of them."**

Hebrews 8:10-11

God did it for His own sake.

"I, even I, am He who blots out your transgressions for **My own sake;** and I will not remember your sins."

Isaiah 43:25

"...This is the heritage of the servants of the Lord, and **their righteousness is from Me."**

Isaiah 54:17b

"For I will be merciful to their unrighteousness, and their sins and their lawless deeds **I will remember no more."**

Hebrews 8:12

IT IS A LISTENING COVENANT

While the old covenant is based on doing things right outwardly, the new covenant requires more in that it demands an open and honest heart. It is based on obedience from the heart.

The old covenant said, "Thou shall not kill" and "Thou shall not commit adultery." But the new covenant requires that God has total control of our hearts. Not only should we not kill, but we must not have the motive to kill. Not only should we not commit adultery, but we must let God cleanse our evil motives.

"You have heard that it was said to those of old, 'You shall not murder,' and whoever murders will be in danger of the judgment. But I say to you that whoever is angry with his brother without a cause shall be in danger of the judgment."

Matthew 5:21-22

"You have heard that it was said to those of old, 'You shall not commit adultery.' But I say to you that whoever looks at a

woman to lust for her has already committed adultery with
her in his heart."

(vs. 27-28)

The good news is that God has given us a new
heart. We cannot please Him with our heart of flesh, but
He has put a new heart within us. Our old heart couldn't
live for Him, but our new heart can. "I will give them a
new heart to know Me." Jeremiah 24:7

"Then I will give them one heart, and I will put a new spirit
within them, and take the stony heart out of their flesh, and
give them a heart of flesh."

Ezekiel 11:19

Because of the new covenant, we no longer try to
do something **for** God. Rather we let Him do things
through us. Our life unto God is not a **performance**, but a
response. We live by listening and responding to the Holy
Spirit. We live in availability to Him.

GOD IS THE INITIATOR

We can take no credit for our relationship in the
blood covenant. We did not choose God, He chose us!

"You did not choose Me, but I chose you and appointed you
that you should go and bear fruit, and that your fruit should
remain, that whatever you ask the Father in My name He may
give you."

John 15:16

"Therefore I have said to you that no one can come to Me
unless it has been granted to him by My Father."

John 6:65

Every step we take in the Christian life can be
fruitful only as we allow God to be the initiator. We
cannot get excited about our plans for God, but we **can**
get excited about His plans for us.

154

DESTINY, NOT HISTORY

When Jesus told Simon (Peter) to let down the nets for a catch, Peter's first response was typical. He talked about his past history! "Master, we have toiled all night and caught nothing." Luke 5:5 Most of us bring up the past when God speaks to us. Like Peter, we bring up our previous failures. But God is not interested in our past. He is not interested in where we've been, but where we are going. He is not talking about our history, but our destiny. Anytime God gives us a command, He is talking about our **destiny.**

Peter brought himself out of the trap of reasoning which would have quenched what the Lord wanted to do. Reasoning paralyzes us from moving in God. At first He probably felt like saying, "Lord, you stick to preaching and we'll stick to fishing." But thank God he chose to obey and responded, "...Nevertheless at Your word I will let down the net." (vs. 5) Obedience always cancels out our negative expectations. Don't weigh it, obey it!

Jesus was teaching the new covenant reality. Responding to His initiative brings results. As soon as they obeyed, they caught so many fish that the net was breaking, and they had to call for help from the other boats.

The reasoning mind is contrary to the Holy Spirit. It is hostile to the mind of God. (Romans 8:7) Usually we disobey because what God is saying seems unreasonable. But we forget that God is creative, and whenever He speaks to us He is calling into being something that does not yet exist.

THE FOUNDATION OF THE NEW COVENANT

When Jesus asked the disciples "But who do you say

that I am?" Peter blurted out, "You are the Christ, the Son of the living God." Matthew 16:15-16

The **way** Peter got this information is the foundation of the new covenant. Peter heard from God! God is building His church not on flesh and blood efforts, but by His people hearing the voice of the Father.

> "...Blessed are you, Simon Bar-Jonah, **for flesh and blood has not revealed this to you, but My Father who is in heaven.** And I also say to you that you are Peter, and on this rock I will build My church and the gates of Hades shall not prevail against it."
>
> (vs. 17-18)

This rock, or revelation, the experience of hearing the Father speak to us, by opening our understanding, is the only way God's church is built. That is why the highest priority in our lives must be to know God and desire Him and experience daily communication and fellowship with Him.

All fleshly efforts must be crucified, and we must draw nigh unto Him. "Unless the Lord builds the house, they labor in vain who build it..." Psalm 127:1

Jesus said, "My sheep hear My voice, and I know them and they follow Me." John 10:27 He didn't say "My sheep listen to tapes and get involved in great ministries."

Too many ministers are too busy to hear God. They are spending all their time in administration. But what can we give to people if we have not spent time in God's presence?

FAILURE-PROOF

The new covenant cannot fail, because God has designed it to be dependent upon Himself, not on our precision performance.

"Thus God, determining to show more abundantly to the heirs of promise the immutability of His counsel, confirmed it by an oath, that by two immutable things, in which it is impossible for God to lie, we might have strong consolation..."

Hebrews 6:17-18

It is a heart covenant. If we keep our hearts right before Him, He will be faithful to make up for the lacks in our endeavors to walk before Him. We must walk before Him, willingly letting Him shine His light into the depths of our being, for He is a God who tries and tests the motives of the heart (Hebrews 4:12).

David spoke prophetically when he wrote,

"The steps of a good (righteous) man are ordered by the Lord, and He delights in his way. Though he fall, he shall not be utterly cast down; for the Lord upholds him with His hand." Psalm 37:23-24

God has a **clause** built into the covenant! "Though he fall, he shall not be utterly cast down..." God is still faithful to hold us up, even when we fall. He will redeem any mistake as long as we keep our hearts pure before Him. It is a failure-proof covenant! It is good news!

Order Form

Please Send Me:

_____ copies of YOU CAN'T USE ME TODAY, LORD...I DON'T FEEL SPIRITUAL ($6.00 each)

_____ copies of ENJOYING GOD OTHER RARE EVENTS ($3.00 each)

_____ copies of DON'T TALK TO ME NOW, LORD...I'M TRYING TO PRAY ($4.00 each)

_____ copies of MEDICINE FOR THE MIND pamphlet (5 for $1.00)

_____ copies of PRAISE AND WORSHIP pamphlet (5 for $1.00)

_____ Catalog of Cassette Tapes

I am enclosing _____ plus $1.00 for postage and handling.

(Quantity orders over 10 books receive a 20% discount)

Mr./Mrs./Miss _____

Address _____

City _____

State _____ Zip Code _____

Order From:

Steve Sampson
P.O. Box 36324
Birmingham, Alabama 35236